MONASTERY
OF THE
MIND

Edward Leigh

MONASTERY OF THE MIND

A pilgrimage with St Ignatius

ST PAULS

Cover design: DX Imaging

ST PAULS Publishing
187 Battersea Bridge Road, London SW11 3AS, UK
www.stpaulspublishing.com

Copyright © 2012 ST PAULS-UK

ISBN: 978-0-85439-813-3

A catalogue record is available for this book from the British Library.

Set by ST PAULS
Printed by Melita Press, Malta

ST PAULS is an activity of the priests and brothers of the Society of St Paul who proclaim the Gospel through the media of social communication.

CONTENTS

FOREWORD

This is an outstanding book, very timely in an age when there is a wide-spread longing to find meaning in life, along with a fear that perhaps the churches are not delivering that meaning. Edward Leigh introduces the reader, especially perhaps the reader who is not at all sure about "all this religious faith business", to the Spiritual Exercises of Ignatius Loyola. A master-touch is that the journey into Ignatius (and towards God) is set against the refreshingly human background of a family holiday with squabbling children in the car, a physical journey through the places where Ignatius Loyola went; and it makes for a most engaging narrative.

The reader will often nod in appreciation "Yes – I've been there too", and that is the strength of this book, written by a busy layperson to explain how other busy professionals, men and women, can find meaning in their lives with a small addition of spiritual discipline in making these "Spiritual Exercises", and a great deal of encounter with the God who is the deepest reality of all.

This is a book that speaks to the needs of our time. It is, as the author says, "a very human story", short and accessible, "an airport saint, the sort of life you would read when waiting for a train or going off on a short plane journey". It is not a piece of "top-down piety", but comes from the pen of one who knows what it is not to believe. Again and again the reader will be struck by the sheer accessibility of the encounter with God, and will find himself or herself muttering, "If this happened to Edward Leigh, then why not me?" He produces an excellent phrase, one that will speak to many: "reading the gospel every day and returning to it as an actor in the drama through the day".

There is a touch of unmistakable authenticity about this book, with the all-too-familiar rebellion of children on holiday, and the difficulty that people find in praying or being "religious". The author describes himself, in a telling phrase, as "a religious person who found difficulty believing in God".

Father Nicholas King SJ
Oxford University

PROLOGUE

The greatest question all of us face is whether we believe in God. This book is another attempt to answer that question. It is not philosophy. It asks this eternal question through the homely medium of one person encountering the life of one saint on his spiritual journey through life, by way of an actual journey.

It is then three things: a story about a modern family and their very ordinary travels; a story about a remarkable historical person, and a story about a spiritual journey. What my conclusion is on the question I have posed – does God exist? – I shall give at the end.

How to sum up the countless millions of words for the existence of God and about religion over the last three or four thousand years of recorded human history? Whether you are a believer or not, every spiritual writer has eventually centred on the power of meditation; emptying one's mind of all the extraneous clutter that invades it. Draining one's consciousness of every regret of the past, every worry about the future. No one denies that through this process something quite wonderful happens. You are taken out of yourself – one views the ego in perspective. One's very self, the soul of one's being, is invaded with a feeling of peace and contentment. To the believer, this is where one finds God. To the non-believer, the calm essence of the human mind.

Even as a boy I would sometimes get this feeling. I felt myself going down a chute into some other state of being. I could not explain it. But everyone can encounter this sensation in their lives, if they will only seek it out. The question is, do they seek it?

Why are we so stressed? Why do we continue to inflict hurt on ourselves, to disrupt our contentment? And why do whole communities and nations magnify the hurt into hatred between religions, nations and races, so that in the twentieth century whole peoples were traumatised and even destroyed? We have lost the will to try and find this inner contentment. Regardless of race or religion, we all feel. This is the one unifying factor that binds us all.

The point of this book is to suggest that we cannot do this on our own. In everything important in life we seek a guide, we are prepared to learn. Why not in this? Of course we can sit in a quiet wood, contemplate a blade of grass, and make some progress, but soon we will reach a plateau, a plain of dryness. The thoughts of the world will invade us and we will be back where we started.

Shouldn't we be prepared to look at the spiritual masters of previous ages? They have all dwelt on this theme: the Buddha, Jesus, Mohammed, their followers and their saints.

Many people say they believe in God but are "not religious" – they reject organised religion as a man – made set of rules. My problem has always been the opposite. I have never been absolutely sure that God exists, but I am religious. I find that when I go to church, I feel good. I find help in locating this peaceful and satisfying centre of my existence.

St Ignatius is just one spiritual guide I can learn from. If anyone non-religious remembers him now, it is as the founder of the Jesuits, a religious Order that imposed a certain dogma they find hard to accept. But it is for that very reason he is interesting. At the core of his teaching was a strong spiritual insight we can all understand. This book is about a spiritual journey, but it is also about an actual journey, therefore it is a very human story.

This book is not primarily for the believer. It is for someone, like most people today, mildly anxious and inquiring, a sceptic about the very existence of God. Do you believe in God, as an intelligent designer of the place where you are? Do you have doubts about whether He cares about you? You are like most people in the modern world. This book asks you to create a place apart in your mind: a monastery, with no physical presence, where you can confront the divine or this divine question.

You may have been attracted by books that tell you to free the mind of thoughts of the past and the future. This is useful, but do you find that it is not enough? Is not our humanity in our thought? How then can we shut it out? What is a monastery? A place where you work, attend services, read spiritually. Is this too much for you? Think again.

Your work you already have, but do you have no time to stop for a second and put it in relation to the divine services? Somewhere there will be a service on – not just on Sunday but every day. Why not go to it? Take time out from the day. Do you waste your time reading stuff that makes you depressed and frustrated? Start by reading the life of a saint. This is one such life.

INTRODUCTION

I cannot be certain when I first got my idea to write a book about St Ignatius, but perhaps it was at Mass that day. It occurred to me, as I was listening to the readings about him, how useful it would be if we had some more short books about how saints used to live their lives.

Perhaps I was angry that day, or inquiring, or sad. It doesn't matter. The door of the church stood open. I entered to find a way forward for my unbelief. By chance, the Mass was for St Ignatius of Loyola's day. I listened. What was intriguing about this saint was that he had lived a very ordinary and selfish life. A shattering, literally shattering event changed his life. He devoted the rest of his life to seeking God.

I decided I would like to find out more about him. Of course I tried first to read about him. Nothing was very satisfactory, but I started to learn more. I noticed that most 'religious' books are written for religious people who 'believe'. Faith is assumed. What if, like in me, doubts persisted? Would it be useful to have a guide for the unbeliever towards belief? Could one way be to base it on a life of a saint? Would such a book be useful?

As I wander around looking for books to read, sometimes before an aeroplane or train journey, I am constantly struck by just how little there is to read which is uplifting, which fulfils some sort of spiritual need, which actually does something positive for people. There are just row upon row of cheap, pulp novels or endless magazines and newspapers which don't really do a lot for me. Occasionally I would prefer to read about the lives of saints. But are the saints really relevant to our time? Many people think not; they see them as boring and irrelevant to modern life. Of course, there is a heroic quality about their lives which is quite remarkable, and, after all, we do live in an age where people are seeking something that they can't get from the ordinary world.

Perhaps, like many people nowadays, you have dipped into the odd book on New Age spirituality; perhaps you have even tried some of it out. Perhaps you also found it unsatisfying, just as Ignatius began to find the knightly romances he had been in the habit of reading unsatisfying. If so, you may be surprised by what a heroic sixteenth-century Spanish Catholic can give you.

What do I mean by calling him 'heroic'? Heroism for me means courage, perseverance, loyalty and willpower – qualities that don't necessarily shape the lives of modern celebrities. These traditional 'heroic' qualities stand in stark contrast to the modern icons of money, image and status. The saints were usually utterly unknown to the wider world in their lifetime and disregarded. They were poor. Their image – if they had one – was one of failure, not success. Attempting to lead and follow the life of a saint is a fight back against trivial modern values. This is what this book is about.

When it comes to material things, many of us have everything we need – such wonderful prosperity, fairly long lives – lives which are good enough to do everything that we really want to do, and most of us live them in good health. Yet, there is always the great unanswered question: what is it all for, where does it all lead? The lives of the saints can tell us something fresh about the modern world, even though people like Ignatius lived so long ago. Some of what he wrote is so difficult to read.

His life in sixteenth century Spain is impossibly remote to our times. Yet, the more one gets into it, the more one realises that it is relevant to our present needs and he has indeed much to tell us. So that is why, sitting in Mass, I decided to write a book about St Ignatius.

I had got into the habit of going to Mass in Westminster Cathedral on most days. My wife, Mary, took the children off to school and I was left with the smallest one, Theodore, to whom I read stories (if I could persuade him not to watch television). When I first woke up, I would throw on my tracksuit and run the few blocks up Horseferry Road, past Vincent Square to the Cathedral, arriving there out of breath for the 8am Mass. At first I could stay till Communion and run back. Then, Nicholas, my second son, had to be in school by 8:50 am, so I could stay only for the Gospel reading and the short sermon. I began to like these informal Masses with no pomp, no singing and no elaboration, for they are over in twenty-five minutes. The best part for me is the silence after Communion. Of course, one can be silent and pray at home, but it seems to me to have more force if one sits in church knowing that everyone else is sending up a prayer as well. Perhaps it is also because one is in the presence of the Blessed Sacrament – but then the non-religious would view that as a tediously pious thought. All this time I still doubted; but I wanted to learn more.

That day, on the feast of St Ignatius, at the start of Mass the priest gave a brief potted history of Ignatius' life. As I sat, I wanted there and then to find out more about him. Of course, dozens of learned books have already been written about Ignatius, most of them very long, and very unreadable and most were written in another age. The lives of saints used to be the usual fare for someone wanting to do a little reading at home. But, perhaps today people are put off by the lavish praises showered on the saints. Or they feel that these men and women, who died so long ago, have little relevance today. I wanted to write something short and accessible which gave a feel for the man. So the idea was something along the lines of an 'airport saint', the sort of life you would read whilst waiting for a train or going off on a short plane journey.

People ask me why I didn't just attempt to write a life of St Ignatius. I tell them that this has been done many times before and by people, mainly Jesuits, far more scholarly than myself. There is no need for more hagiography about him. I wanted to help people who never go to a religious bookshop and to do so by approaching St Ignatius in three stages. After all, a three-in-one story is not entirely contrary to a Christian message. This would be a personal spiritual journey of one unbeliever prepared to believe – me. Secondly, it would be the story of a saint's life and how he helped me. Thirdly, it would be the story of how this journey impacted on my family.

That was the idea that occurred to me sitting in Mass that summer's morning. So far, so good. I then had to get on with the difficult part. I got all the books I could find about his life and started reading. That was easy enough. Writing, though, was hard. I could not come to grips with the man. So, after a few months of desperate writing, I decided to take my family on a trip to Spain to seek him out 'face to face'. I did not warn the children about the purpose of my trip – there would have been a rebellion. I just said, 'Why don't we drive to Spain?' and they all agreed! How little they knew..

Meditation: Introduction

This book is written for those of little faith. The more unbelieving or sceptical you are, the more you might enjoy or need this book. In a moment, I will give you a reading to think about.

Fall into an inner consciousness and put yourself in the presence of your inner self, your soul. If you have faith in God, put your trust in Him. If not, in that part of your being that might always be. That part of extraordinary wonder. Your mind, your inner self.

Now look at your fellow human beings anew. Not at their ugliness or irritating habits. Look beneath their skin. Imagine them having much the same thoughts, fears, wants and desires as you. You are they, to some extent, a lot more than you think, and they are you for countless millennia back into history and forward into the future.

If you prefer, you can read this book just as a biography of St Ignatius, the chapters about his life are in chronological order and clearly marked. It's a good story on its own. However, if you want to go a bit deeper, bear with me.

Read this book slowly and see what the life of a saint means to you. Above all, start to think how you are going to talk to God. This is what prayer is, as well as being prepared to take time to listen to Him. A daunting prospect: 'I don't know how to pray,' you say. There is one way, the obvious way. Go somewhere quiet. Re-collect yourself.

Consciously think of yourself as coming into the presence of God. Rid your mind as much as possible of the past and the future. Be aware only of the present moment.

Concentrate on a single thing. Perhaps ask God for help with something now, with an anxiety or something causing unhappiness.

Breathe slowly. Calm yourself physically from the head down. Repeat a phrase slowly over and over again. "Jesus, have mercy on me, a sinner." Or say nothing. Place your thoughts with God. Don't expect an answer straight away, or perhaps at all. Invite into yourself a feeling of calm, or of acceptance.

Now gently come back into the real world. Or is it real?

Finally, end the prayer with the sign of the cross, a bow or just a word, if you are in a busy place or shy.

That is one sort of prayer. Many of you will be familiar with it. But there is another, and this is where Ignatius comes in. He asks us to place ourselves, I repeat, ourselves, within the Gospels.

So we meditate on one scene. We feel it, see it and hear it. We are there. We are an actor, or at least a listener, within the scene. We read it two or three times until we are totally familiar with it. Every word, every scene becomes pregnant with emotion. Shall we start with a scene?

I was given this at a short retreat at St Beuno's, the Jesuit Spirituality Centre, but others may occur to you.

John was standing with two of his disciples; and he looked at Jesus as he walked, and said, "Behold, the Lamb of God!" The two disciples heard him say this, and they followed Jesus. Jesus turned, and saw them following, and said to them, "What do you seek?" John 1:35-38.

This question is addressed to you.

What do you seek? What do you believe in? What is it that you want out of life?

These are questions we all ask. They are questions this book seeks to address.

Like all of us, you seek happiness, but happiness is closure. Suffering follows joy, which follows suffering eternally. Real joy can never be based on things of this world, because they are transitory. But, when someone tells you that real joy can be found only in God, you doubt, or are full of doubts, about whether God exists. The things of this world – health, human love, fame, power, possessions, holidays – may be transitory but they at least exist, if only for a short time. God may be for eternity, but He may not be at all. Remember, I am not asking you to accept anything on trust. This is an exercise, a spiritual exercise. Trust to faith, if not faith in God, then faith in the exercise, as a means of seeking God.

The vital first step is to accept that complete joy can never be found in possessions. Even love rooted in a family is ephemeral. It is ultimately cut short by death. You want to seek a deeper, more resilient joy.

The Spiritual Exercises of St Ignatius are something we shall look at later in the book. Shall we start with a simpler, easier one of our own? I am not asking you to accept Jesus as God. Let's just think of Him as a great teacher, a holy man. Shall we meditate on His life theme by theme and see what it does for us? I will give you meditations throughout this book based on a journey.

St Ignatius created his 'Spiritual Exercises' first. The Jesuits, his 'Company' (in the military sense) of Jesus came later. His aim was to open up souls to God. His was an age where indifference had set in, where far too many priests went through the motions of mumbling an inaudible Mass. Unusually for the time, he went out into the streets dressed as a beggar – indeed he was one. He talked to people in their own language. He asked those he talked to at any length to use scenes from the Gospel as a spiritual exercise, imagining they were in them, sharing the hope of Jesus' mission, His Passion, and His Resurrection,

You may not be ready for that in its entirety yet, but you feel the need for something, just as society wants for something more. So, for a moment, follow the life of a fellow seeker. If you wish, reject his ideas after you have taken an afternoon to read of his quest.

Nothing will be lost. You may come to the conclusion that you can no longer walk alone, that you need a guide. That following a guide need not be restrictive; you can leave him any time. You can take the decision to tie yourself to him, or you can slip the knot at any time with a gentle tug, but you can no longer live in indifference and depression. You must seek.

PART ONE

Chapter I
Our Journey into Spain

We went by a rather roundabout route. First, my wife's sister had offered to put us up for a few days in the French Alps and I couldn't resist that. Then a total solar eclipse was scheduled for 11th August and I couldn't resist that either, although it meant driving up North back to the Vosges. I camped along with everyone else. It was a fun thing to do, although, at the moment of the eclipse, an enormous black cloud came along and obscured everything. It just felt as if we were in twilight.

The next day we packed our tent and crammed everything into the car, which wasn't easy to do, as we have six children. We were like four squabbling couples: Mary and I squabbled; the two eldest girls, Natalia, thirteen, and Tamara, twelve, squabbled; Benedict, ten, and Marina, nine, squabbled; and lastly, Nicholas, four, and Theodore, two, squabbled. Well, they didn't squabble, they just hit each other. With so many, we couldn't afford to stay in hotels, so we camped. That meant three tents; sleeping bags; clothes; food; cutlery and books; maps, buckets (and accumulated dust and sand); pieces of paper – everything had to fit into the car. It did but only with a lot of heaving, and it took four or five hours to get the show on the road.

The Toyota Previa Space Wagon, year on year, got more and more battered as we bumped into other cars and they bumped into us. The situation was made worse, because Mary always insisted on owning up when we bumped other people – like the time that Benedict released the handbrake, and decided to drive the car off himself – whereas so often, other people don't own up when they hit us!

So we left our camp site in the Vosges, and headed south. It was a day of blistering heat, and we took shelter at Besançon. Should we press on, or take shelter for the night south of Lyons? We pressed on through the night, waking the children up at 1.30am to walk around the ramparts of Carcassonne. We had been there twenty-five years before, when it had been rather quiet. Now it's overrun by tourists, and perhaps the best time to appreciate it is at 1.30 in the morning, when the noisy cafes and discos have finally closed, and one can walk around the old town alone and in peace.

The next stop was Lourdes, where we were to stay for two days. I wanted to do a recce for an idea I had of a family pilgrimage with the children. I arrived in the morning, to be welcomed with open arms by Madame Rouglon, the owner of St Catherine's Hotel. She had looked after Mary and me when we came together on a youth pilgrimage with the Order of Malta Volunteers. Long discussions followed as to who was to sleep where. We finally squeezed into two of the tiny rooms that one always finds in Lourdes. They must be the smallest hotel rooms in the world, and with the smallest showers.

Those who have never been to Lourdes cannot understand it. Visitors crowd the narrow streets of this old town, which 'nestles at the foot of the Pyrenees', as the guide book puts it. Lourdes is big business, with more hotels than any other French town outside Paris. Some people are put off by the souvenir shops with their endless rows of plastic Madonnas and leave in a hurry. They should persevere and walk down into the *Domaine*, where the processions take place from the basilica, perched on its rock above the grotto. Here, all commerce is banned. The crowds are enormous, yet quiet and reverent, and there is an extraordinary atmosphere in the place, especially by the Grotto, where St Bernadette said that she saw the Virgin.

We did all the usual Lourdes things with our children, including taking them for a holy bath, which is very refreshing – there is something very powerful about a cold bath with spiritual overtones on a hot day. The baths are beyond the Grotto, where, after St Bernadette claimed that the Virgin appeared to her, a spring appeared. The water is collected, and one can also be immersed in it. Historically, sick people hoped thereby to be cured of their maladies. The miracle of Lourdes is not so much the physical cures, which are very rare, but the miracle of faith that is enhanced for most people who go there.

I took the children swimming in the *Lac de Lourdes*, and walked up the rustic path to the field and small barn where St Bernadette herded her sheep as a girl. I climbed the hill to the tiny *cachot*, formerly the town gaol, where she was brought up after her father fell into penury. The children and Mary carried on into the fort within the chateau. I went back down into the town and wandered around looking for a quiet coffee on my own.

One evening, we went on the torchlight procession, holding our candles high and singing *Ave Maria*. The children, of course, got bored and ran off somewhere.

We trudged in the heat, in the Blessed Sacrament procession, and three times a day we had our meals in the hotel. Mary has a theory that all the hotels in Lourdes are connected by an underground tunnel, because all the meals appear to be exactly the same. One's main memory is of chicken and chips and lots of bread; weak coffee served out of a jug at breakfast; and bottles of red wine left on one's table with its white cloth. At least the food is plentiful and cheap. The value at these hotels is superb. I had been a little worried about taking the children to Lourdes but they seemed to quite enjoy it. I suppose, in a sense, to them it was like Venice, which was also quite a successful visit for my family a few years before. It was one of the first theme parks in history.

What is particularly amazing about Lourdes is the vast numbers of people milling about, largely in silence, by the Grotto on the side of the fast-flowing river Gave, which is still almost a mountain stream. There is something peaceful about sitting on its opposite bank, looking over it, the sun sparkling on its waters. Over the heads of people sitting by the Grotto are candles in a pyramid, flickering. There are stone benches on the bank. At night the light of the candles dances on the water. Sometimes there is a low murmur as the rosary is being said nearby. It is restful and peaceful. If you're short-sighted, like me, you look at the out-of-focus representation in a little niche above the Grotto of what Bernadette says she saw – the Virgin Mary with her rosary and roses on her feet. Even if one isn't a believer, one can't help but be struck by this vast crowd of people moving silently around.

So that's Lourdes. Time was pressing on and I had work to do. We were now almost at our destination. We were heading for Loyola in the Basque Country, where St Ignatius was born and grew up. I had only a large-scale map of the whole of Spain, but printed on it were the words *'Sanctuario de Loyola'*. What town was it near? I remembered dimly that St Ignatius had been brought up near Azpeitia.

We went into the new country, of course, with no Spanish money – the Visa card having just been rejected at a garage coming out of Lourdes. At a local shop, I gave the card to the attendant. *"Ça ne marche pas"*, he said. He was already in a bad mood. A group of Irish pilgrims, who he said were 'gypsies' had just charged into his shop with numerous children, and his wife stood at the door with her arms crossed, trying to prevent them walking out with bars of chocolate. I asked them if there was a bank nearby where I could change some money. *"Ils sont tout fermés. C'est déjeuner."* After a while, he relented and told me there was a machine in the next village. I asked him if I could drive off and get the money, but there was no trust in his eyes. *"Il faut que vous restez ici."*

What about the other card, I wondered? But the Nat West card didn't work either. I had visions of spending the rest of the day there, serving petrol to pay my debt. I tried a new tack: *"Est-ce-que tu prends un Eurocheque?"* *"Non."* I stayed there and Mary drove off in search of a bank. I asked if I could have a coffee. He brightened up but didn't serve it immediately. The Irish family were leaving and his mood was improving, but there was still an enormous row. The patron as good as accused them of stealing chocolate. He asked for the petrol money. The Irishman produced his card. It didn't work either. Was he going to have to search for a machine, leaving his wife and children as hostage?

He dug into his hip pocket and produced an enormous wodge of French notes. Having established his superiority in the 'ability to pay' stakes, the tables were turned. "This is Lourdes!" he said. "It's supposed to be a holy place! A place where you trust people." He stormed out. His enormous white van, pulling an even larger caravan, shot off.

"Gypsies." said the *garagiste*. "They would steal my entire shop if they could." Suddenly his attitude changed. Something was obviously wrong with the Visa machine. "Was it a coffee you wanted?" he smiled. Would he be so friendly when Mary returned without any money, I wondered. I drank my coffee. Normally in France, an espresso is a delight. This was in a paper cup and had a distinct taste of... washing-up liquid? Mary returned. I walked over. She had the money, thank God! I drove away.

Visiting Lourdes had been such an emotional experience, but the incident at the garage jolted us all back to ordinary life, the life of credit cards and petrol pumps. The motorway now stretched before me. There had been quite a lot of publicity that year about the pilgrimage to Saint Jacques de Compostela, but how were we to find the path? I had produced my map of the whole of France to the girl at St Catherine's Hotel desk; I was met with a blank look. "If you ask Madame, she might know."

The St Catherine's Hotel is a strangely-run place. It is on a corner and Madame Rouglon, the owner, runs it in tandem with the hotel opposite. In theory it is a different hotel but, I suspect, serving the same food on the same day to very much the same sort of clientele. But no complaints and all was done with great charm. A finger hovered over Saint-Pied-de-Port on my large scale map. "I think the walkers start there."

Should I set the six children down at the foot of the Pyrenees and *make* them walk over there? Maybe another year. (Three years later I did precisely that.) I thought they were perhaps still just a little too young to walk several hundred miles in pursuit of St Jacques. As I bombed along the Autoroute, a sign appeared: *'AIRE DE HASTINGS, EXPOSITION DE ST JACQUES DE COMPOSTELA'*. I stopped, of course, and the children rushed in. They found a map of Europe beneath their feet. In the exhibition, scenes of medieval life flashed before six very modern children. A medieval world, in which most people never travelled more than thirteen miles from their home in their entire lives; because that was the furthest you could walk in a day and still return home to bed. Could we ever understand the simple faith and the superstitions of that time?

My guide book to Spain said that never had so glorious a shrine as the one at Compostela been erected in the name of so preposterous a story. I thought that rather a cynical attitude, but one could never understand the medieval era of Faith in the clinical atmosphere of a modern exhibition at the side of a motorway. The picture of the pilgrim with the cockle shell on his hat was detached and distant. They used to wear the cockles that they collected on the Finisterre Coast of Spain after finishing their pilgrimage. How could we understand the poverty, the dirt, the disease, the tiredness, the thirst and the hunger they lived with on the many days of their journey?

So those were some of the simple adventures I enjoyed in my short journey from Lourdes into Spain. Luckily, no-one asked me for any money, as I didn't have any. We were speeding along the auto-vista in northern Spain when I decided on my plan: I would head straight for Azpeitia.

The motorway came to an end. The toll-gate attendant obligingly accepted the defunct credit card and we started to climb into the mountains. The villages were strangely depressing, in contrast to my preconceptions. Many of the buildings seemed 'newish'. There were small blocks of flats everywhere. I arrived in Azpeitia. The town was shut up – completely empty – despite it being five in the afternoon.

I stopped in a deserted market square. I saw a kind of souvenir stall selling everything from rubber balls to pieces of clothing. "Do you speak English?" "No." *"Tourismo?"* I asked. "Office of Tourism?" A shake of the head.

There was a small boy. He seemed to know a smattering of English. Various complicated directions were given, but the town revealed nothing. We drove on to the *Sanctuario de Loyola* which lies at the end of a long, wide avenue close to the town. I had read so much about it. Eventually it loomed into view. It is a massive baroque building with a large cupola in the middle.

I had come in search of the castle of St Ignatius of Loyola, a sixteenth century knight, but I could see nothing of it. I walked over to what appeared to be a retreat house on the side of the main building. A nun sat at the desk. "Do you speak English?" "No," she replied. "Any chance of staying here?" I asked uselessly. She smiled the smile of a woman who hadn't the faintest idea of what I was talking about.

I walked up to the main building, up some steps and through a door. There was a tiny cubby hole at the end, and there I found Father Jesus Mary. I asked the same question to him, "Do you speak English?" "Yes," he replied. At last here was somebody I could communicate with. "I wonder if you could help me. I am looking for an Office of Tourism. Do you happen to know if there is one open nearby? I need accommodation for my family and myself." "If you go through the door you will find a lady who might be able to help." He gestured towards the end of the corridor.

The door was locked. I had to wait for someone to come out through it. Eventually someone did. The lady who emerged was pleasant and attractive. She gave me lots of brochures. The most promising line of attack seemed to be an *Agro Tourismo*, a villa, farm or cottage available for in the countryside to rent at a reasonable price. I would drive to the Tourist Office closest to me. I walked out and back to the car, where Mary and the kids were waiting.

I was about to get in and drive off when I thought I would ask the nice chap in the cubby hole for help one more time. After all, English-speakers appeared to be so few and far between in Spain. "Is there any chance of a family staying here? Do you have a hostel?" "Yes, there may be. I will ring my friend," he replied. I waited hopefully. "He's not there. I will try again in five minutes." He rang again. Was it five, ten, or fifteen minutes later? "He has gone to see his mother. He will be back late."

My friend seemed to be in no hurry. It was getting on and I had a large family waiting in the car outside. "I have to say Mass at 7pm," continued Father Jesus Mary. "Come back after that. I will meet you on the steps at 7.25pm. The Mass is in Basque." By all this I cottoned on that my friend was a Basque-speaking Jesuit Priest. I walked over to the others and waited for Mass. Time was passing.

The Mass finished. I understood not a word, but the faith of the people was quite extraordinary and they sang their hymns with gusto. Meanwhile, I admired the Baroque beauty of the interior. Father Jesus Mary appeared. I went back to the cubby hole. There was still no answer from his friend, the Director of the Hostel. "I shall show you where there is a restaurant and then I will find you somewhere to stay," he said.

It was getting on. But what was there to do? We had no alternative, and Jesus Mary jumped into the overcrowded dirty car and off we drove. We hurtled into a residential area and ended up in a cross between a Liverpool council estate and a Spanish piazza. The buildings were from Liverpool, the people from Spain, which could be a good or bad combination, depending on one's point of view.

We entered a café in the corner. I ordered a Spanish omelette that was the tiniest I have ever seen. Jesus Mary's piece of toast wasn't much larger. Anyway, we had a jolly meal. I heard all about my friend's family. He never asked about me, what I did, etc. Was he being polite, according to Basque notions of politeness – or was he just not interested?

We went back to the sanctuary in the dark. It was now 10 pm. Jesus Mary muttered something and ran off in some direction or other. Just when I thought I would never see him again, he returned and asked me to follow him. He had the key, and we had somewhere to stay at last. Was it five or six hours after arriving at Azpeitia? It was a hostel in the grounds of the *Sanctuario*. We were camped, the eight of us, in a huge dormitory with twenty-one bunk beds; four lavatories and four showers in an adjoining bathroom. The children were satisfied and so was I, especially at £2 per head per night.

During the interminable wait outside Jesus Mary's little cubby hole I had started to look around me. I was in a corridor, but a corridor, strangely enough, open to the sky. As I looked up, I realized that I was standing next to a sixteenth century tower-castle buried inside the late Baroque building. There was a little sloping cobbled path leading to a door at the front of the castle. This was the castle where Ignatius was born and grew up. The countryside around the castle is not instantly attractive to the eye; the valley itself is broad and flat. On either side, vast rounded hills block any view. The castle is small, no more than a simple tower.

The ground floor is immaculate now, of course. But when St Ignatius was a child, it would have had a rough barn-like feel, and been stuffed with barrels, bottles of wine coming to maturity, and other odds and ends – all the paraphernalia of a large country house. Above the ground floor was the kitchen, where the servants huddled together to sleep. On the second floor lived the Lord of the Manor, Ignatius' father, with his wife. He spent his days next to the chapel, and he ate and slept in the Chamber on the third floor, while the guests and children lived on the fourth floor.

It's all lovingly restored now, and many of the Baroque additions have been stripped away, but the atmosphere is polished and austere, rather like the Headmaster's House of a boarding school – a place for visitors, not a place to be lived in. The ground floor is immaculate, perhaps excessively so, but as one climbs the broad wooden staircase, the house still comes alive. The top floor is dominated by the room, now a chapel, where Ignatius was to have his conversion experience. But no doubt in his boyhood, this too would have been very different. I call him "Ignatius", but really I should, at this stage of his life, call him "Inigo", because that was the name his parents gave him.

Meditation: Journey

Let us journey on our way, and I will go before you. Genesis 33:12.
Rise, let us go hence. John 14:31.

We are constantly on the move. It is fashionable to blame this on "modern" living. But we usually go somewhere for a purpose, just as we have always done. The better way is to use movement for prayer. When we drive on a familiar route, the mind does a sort of automatic prayer anyway. It shifts into automatic mode, so we have little memory of the journey. This is an opportunity for prayer, as is sitting in a traffic jam or on a train. Prayer whilst sitting in a traffic-jam can be a conscious shifting of the mind sideways from the present painful, frustrating reality into separateness, a slowing down of the heart.

People dislike lying awake at night. In fact it's a great opportunity to pray. It's quiet. No disturbance. Free the mind from worries, particularly about money. It's at these times that sometimes I feel this strange sensation of falling into myself, my mind, myself narrowing and falling down into a void within myself.

Contemplation of God brings joy. We need to direct our mind to God regularly throughout the day to ensure our joy.

You don't even have to believe in God in following on the inner road. You are following yourself to the infinite, to the fundamental laws of nature. Every atom of you and everything else is part of the law of the universe, moving ceaselessly in union with everything else.

So how do we free the mind? We need some sort of focus and self-discipline.

Pray five times a day. Pray in the morning on waking and in the middle of the morning. What a lovely idea the Angelus is: at midday stopping, saying the Hail Mary, directing the mind to God. Pray at lunchtime, in the early evening and upon going to bed. Matins, Lauds. Midday Prayer, Vespers, Compline.

How tragic that we have lost the wonderful value of regular prayer during the day. For joy is in the contemplation of God, of the infinite.

Why this feeling of dissatisfaction in us? We fear death. Why can't we realise that we are unique? The greater part of us is exactly the same as other people. We are one part of a unity.

Chapter 2
The Childhood
and Youth of St Ignatius

Inigo was the youngest of thirteen children. His mother Maria died either at his birth or shortly after, which may have been around 1491, making him almost an exact contemporary of Henry VIII, although their careers were to be very different. Inigo himself was never sure exactly when he was born. It is difficult to get into the atmosphere of the house now, but we have to imagine it as it was, filled with servants, and a large family. Inigo would have spoken Basque, a language that makes little sense to anyone else. He was to lose much of it when he went off to Court. But in his earliest years, it would have been the language of his nurse and of those he spent much of his time with. He was named after a saintly Benedictine abbot of the district. Thus the future soldier of Christ was named after a man who practised a very different type of spirituality – the Rule of Saint Benedict – one that I personally find most attractive.

As he was the youngest son, there was no property waiting for him. He had to live by his wits. While still a boy, it was clear that he could no longer stay at home. He had to learn the ways of a gentleman, as did all the young men of his class, the minor nobility. So, he was sent off as a page to the Royal Treasurer; this was life in the Court of the great man. It was a world of privilege and arrogance, of learning to drink and to wench, in other words, a life of pure selfishness. An education which taught beautiful handwriting to someone who could make a career as a Private Secretary to a great man of state, who could ride and fight with a sword, who would make his way in the world of a courtier or as the governor of a castle, or even perhaps of a Province as he grew to great things. It was a world of polite, unquestioning religious observance; a world where the cloak of religion could be quietly dropped as soon as one left the church.

But this was not the eighteenth century world of formal observance on a Sunday and polite agnosticism during the rest of the week. A busy man of affairs would be happy to go to Mass every day, and allow, to some extent, the atmosphere to percolate through his behaviour. It was not a religion of meditation on Gospel narratives. The Mass was celebrated quickly, devoutly said, but barely listened to. Communion was rarely taken. The atmosphere soaked in. Then one moved on. But a gentleman still remembered to be generous to the Church as a benefactor, as indeed, did Inigo's patron, the Royal Treasurer. People nowadays are put off by the formality of religion, but at that time it was accepted as a matter of course.

Inigo grew up with the Treasurer's children. Families of the great and wealthy were large. After all, there was no shortage of servants, or of space. This was not a rustic life in some rural castle. The Treasurer moved with the Court. The Court moved often, as they did in those days, and Inigo moved with it.

What a wonderful opportunity for a growing boy! In these days of parental affection, it seems strange to send a boy away for nine or ten years, that the boy should not attend school, or see his family, but should move around the country with near strangers. Then, it was entirely natural. People were tougher, more self-reliant, and grew up more quickly. However, the education probably instilled in young people of noble birth an arrogance which today we would find insufferable.

We know nothing of the sexual development of such a lad. It probably alternated between physical encounters with the lower classes, and romantic infatuation with the higher. The knightly ideal was one of courtly love, and romances such as *Amadis de Gaul* would have been what stirred young Inigo's imagination, which, judging by his later career, he must have had lots of.

Obviously he was lively, according to the standards of the time. Along with the occasional brawling, Inigo was hauled before the Courts in one particularly unpleasant incident over a woman, and then only saved from punishment by his membership of lower clerical orders. Of course, he had no intention of becoming a priest, but it was common for someone of his status at that time to enter the minor orders.

In 1516 the old King Ferdinand died, and the new King Charles V dismissed his old treasurer, Inigo became ready for the world. He had lost his patron. But Don Juan Velasquez's wife gave him a recommendation to the Duke of Najera. There, on the frontier with France, Inigo might yet find glory.

Meditation: Childhood

Youth and the dawn of life are vanity. Ecclesiastes 11:10.
Whoever does not receive the kingdom of God like a little child shall not enter it. Mark 10:15.

Don't try and think.

Just stay still and open the heart to interior silence.

Now in quietness go back. Return to your childhood.

There is no past of regrets. No problems with money or relationships or ambitions or drive.

You are a child, innocent, open, just you.

You are close to the beating heart of your mother. Safe. Secure. Completely in the present, as a child is.

You are conscious only of this minute's sensation and sounds.

You are breathing and hearing only the patter of rain on the window.

Chapter 3
Young Blood

Inigo was now twenty-five. He was ready to start his career. He made his way to the frontier province of Navarre, close to the Pyrenees and the border with France. It had only recently been captured by the Spaniards, who had overturned the Navarese King, Jean d'Albret. The French eyed the province hopefully. This was clearly going to be a fruitful field of adventure.

Inigo was full of confidence. Followed by some youths, he promptly gave chase, brandishing his sword, and had to be held back from attacking them. On another occasion, Inigo had to be given protection against a rival in love who had threatened to kill him. This was a violent society, but Inigo was not just a young fighter. In fact, he was not a professional soldier, more a young courtier who took part in negotiations following a rebellion against Charles V. He was obviously talented and considered a useful asset in tackling matters of state.

The French, under King Francois I, invaded Navarre, under their General, Andre de Foix. The Spaniards were hopelessly outnumbered. Inigo was summoned from his home with his brother Martin and a hundred men at arms. They made their way to Pamplona on the urgent summons of the Duke of Najera.

Inigo's moment of destiny had arrived. The French were advancing on the town with what passed for great force in those days, about 12-13,000 men, whereas the Duke only had about 3,000 under his control. There could be no doubt about the outcome, and the citizens knew that as well.

When Andre de Foix camped outside the city, he was contacted by the magistrates, who offered to open the town to him, as long as there was no pillaging. Inigo could do nothing to save the town when he arrived, so he made his way, immediately, to the citadel, which was still holding out under its commander, Miguel de Herrera. There was now an urgent discussion. They were clearly outnumbered. Should they surrender? Consistent with his reputation as a brave *hidalgo* or knight, Inigo argued for them to try and hold out until relief could come from the Duke.

Andre de Foix now attacked with his artillery and men for about six hours, pounding the walls with his shot. Inigo was in the thick of the fighting, and by all accounts, was a brave example to his men.

Finally, he was struck down by a cannon ball that passed between his legs. His right leg was very severely broken, indeed shattered, and the left leg wounded as well. Once the men saw that Inigo had fallen, the fight went out of them and the citadel fell. Inigo was lucky. He was treated well by the French, his wounds were looked after, his leg was not amputated. However, for those days, this was a serious break. It was May 1521.

Although he didn't know it at the time, that cannon ball that wounded Inigo so severely was to change the course of history – because it changed his life. He was never to fight as a soldier again. He left Pamplona, not the proud hidalgo riding to the rescue of a town with his own kinsmen and men at arms, but carried out of the city, a broken and sick man in a litter on the start of a long and painful journey back home to the Basque country. His home was some seventy miles away.

Meditation: Youth – love the moment

The first commandment is, 'Hear, O Israel: The Lord our God, the Lord is one; and you shall love the Lord your God with all your heart, and with all your soul, and with all your mind, and with all your strength.' The second is this, 'You shall love your neighbour as yourself.' There is no other commandment greater than these. (Mark 12:29-31).

The reading we all try and live by, and fail to do so, is the one in which a scribe approaches Jesus and asks which is the first commandment. Jesus answered,

How difficult I find this, how easy in theory! How can we always love people we are jostled into in the ebb and flow of daily life? How can we love them as ourselves?

I think an easier path to this most demanding of rules is to start by loving the moment. Wherever we are, whenever people or things irritate us, when problems come bubbling to the surface – love the moment. This might be a good thing for you to try. We may not always be able to love our neighbour but we can love this moment, or try to live this moment as fully as possible. This is not just a vague exercise that we can or should divorce from our ordinary life. It is fundamental to it.

This week I awoke, as one does, depressed about what I had achieved in my life. Young people, of course, never have these regrets. Young Inigo certainly didn't. He was just a young hidalgo. He fought, he had mistresses, we presume. He was a romantic. He daydreamed. After his conversion he learned to live in the moment. Young people, in a sense, live in the moment because they are more impulsive and spontaneous than the old. But the spiritual insight that Inigo received at his conversion would have enabled him to live in the moment in a more complete way. If you are a little older, you might try living more as a young person for the moment.

We never know where our work will take us, what achievements lie hidden from the world as we see it today. The phrase 'I must be about my father's business' ran round my head, as phrases do when we are half-asleep. Better to think along these lines than to worry about paying the mortgage.

Chapter 4
Our Visit to Pamplona

My family and I made our way over the mountains from the Basque country to Pamplona. Not walking or riding as Inigo would have done, but in a car, climbing ever higher, and finally down into the plain where Pamplona stands to this day, a very different town to what it was then. It is a northern, civilised and prosperous Spanish city, full of smart shops. It is famous now, of course, for the Bull Run, and when you walk down the streets, there are constant reminders of the bravery of the local youth as they try and avoid the horns of the bulls, and some pictures in the windows of shops which one can show the children, images of bulls rampaging through crowds of young people.

I had a job to do though. I was following in the footsteps of St Ignatius. So I made my way up to the remains of the old citadel. There is a bar up there near the ramparts, and one can look across the plain and get an idea of what it must have been like when this was a medieval town entirely surrounded by walls, besieged by the French. But was this the spot where Inigo had fallen, here on the ramparts which still survive?

It must have been a terrifying experience waiting and watching as the great army approached the utterly inadequate and demoralised garrison. Of course, I had no real idea. I went into the café and asked, and they didn't have any idea either. But they did show me a guide book, and that gave me a few clues.

I retraced my steps through the town and, after wandering around in vain, I finally came across a beggar sitting on the pavement. Whilst pausing for a moment, wondering whether to give him any money, I looked down and, to my astonishment and joy, there was a plaque in the pavement which said that this was the spot where Inigo had fallen five centuries before. It is right in the middle of the town, near the main piazza, although there is no sign of the ramparts, or any view of where the French would have been. Standing by the plaque one looks across to a smart women's boutique and next door is a church which commemorates St Ignatius. The French, along with the walls, have vanished, and one could be anywhere, in a modern city choked with traffic.

I doubt if one person in a hundred walking down that sophisticated modern boulevard notices the plaque or spares a thought for Inigo. Not one in ten thousand would visualise the exhausted and vanquished soldiers crouching on the stricken walls, staring at defeat and surrender or death. They are forgotten. But I had found where he fell. My day in Pamplona was over. I had wandered around the ramparts, the children had bought some wonderful sweets, I had looked at the sites and I had sat in the Cathedral for a time.

I drove back along the motorway and through the mountains for a swim in the sea in the early evening. Inigo's journey would have been very different. It must have been agonising as he took perhaps the best part of a month trying to skirt the enemy, carried on a litter with no pain killers, his leg horribly broken and shattered by a cannon ball, before he finally made it back home alive but desperately ill in June 1521. It was the end of his military career. By the time he got back, the slow journey had ruined the setting of the bones. But at least he was home, in the castle now run by his older brother Martin.

Meditation: Visit

God will visit you. Genesis 50:24.
Thou visitest the earth and waterest it. Psalm 65:9.
I was sick and you visited me, I was in prison and you came to me.
Matthew 25:36.

Sometimes we search for something in vain, and some off-chance happening prompts us to find it.

In Pamplona I searched in vain for any sign of St Ignatius. It was in turning to and talking to a beggar that I saw it.

You may also try giving up your normal search and let something simply happen to you. Or try observing: observe things more closely to see what is really going on around you.

We journey often. But how often do we visit each other?

The word "visit" is a lovely word. It conjures up "The Visitation", when the Virgin Mary visited her cousin Elizabeth once she has heard that she is to conceive a baby. Indeed, the first thing she does is to go on a visit.

Whom do we know that we have not visited recently? A friend or relation perhaps? Why not try phoning someone you have not talked to in a long time.

Chapter 5
The Conversion

It was, no doubt, swelteringly hot in the small family castle as Inigo lay on his couch, where today one can sit in the chapel. Medicine was primitive, especially in an obscure rustic village. The doctors had set his broken bones, but they were set badly, and had to be broken and re-set – again, of course, with no pain-killers. Inigo, as a true knight, uttered not a word of complaint, only clenching his fist, something which was allowed.

Hope was fading. Fever took hold and the last rites were administered. An appeal, as was customary, no doubt, in such cases, was made to St Peter, and Inigo began to recover. It was the feast of St Peter and St Paul, June 29 1521. The appeal to Peter, one of his favourite saints, had apparently worked. But worse was to come.

His bones were deformed. This was insufferable to the vanity of a knight who spent his life in stockings. He asked to have the part of the badly-set bone which was now protruding cut off with a saw, and again, through the excruciating agony, he uttered not a word. This of course had nothing to do with any religious conviction, and everything to do with pride. How could he fight or dance (his two passions) with a gammy leg?

Eventually, he was on the mend. The time passed desperately slowly. He asked for romances to read. There were none. In a small castle such as this, there was no book in the house, save *A Life of Christ* and *A Life of the Saints*. He had no choice but to read them. He pondered them, particularly the lives of St Dominic and St Francis. St Francis was a man like himself, of good family, obtaining his happiness with a life of selfishness. A strange thing happened to St Francis. He realised that his quest for glory left him feeling depressed. Similarly, as Inigo lay there, he began to feel that his old life had been empty.

Part of my interest in religion comes from the same feeling. So much secular reading, watching and listening leaves me cold, or worse, depressed. Reading in a religious vein may be a struggle to start, like attempting a painting. But it never leaves me depressed.

During the week that I stayed at Loyola, I used to go up to Inigo's old room every day and sit there. I tried to put myself into his mind as he lay on his couch, I tried to think of myself being in pain, bored, trying to pass the time, reading about the life of the saints, and of Christ, and I began to feel that I was understanding him in a way that I couldn't by just sitting at home reading about him.

As the months passed, Inigo saw a new challenge appearing. He would be a different sort of knight, braver because he was poorer, more whole because ultimately, he would be destitute. He would fight on behalf of Christ the King, rather than the king of Spain. He pondered the life of St Dominic, whom he came to admire for his energy. He read about St Onofrio, who had retired to the desert as a hermit. Then a strange thing happened. As he lay there, he was day-dreaming. No doubt he often dreamt of his old life: of his dreams of glory, and of the future. But as he did so, these dreams left him not disgusted, but less and less happy. Whilst he day-dreamed about the saints in this obscure book written by a Dominican, Jacopo de Voragine, which would be unreadable to us nowadays, something happened: he felt happy, elated. As I was sitting in his room five centuries later, I too tried to imagine what he must have been thinking.

It is a strange fact that if one makes a similar effort to think about the lives of saints or any spiritual matter, one can also get this feeling of well-being. One doesn't find it in thinking about the ways of the world.

Inigo's life was changing. He was undergoing what we now call a "conversion experience". He even had a vision or "dread" that he saw the Virgin Mary, but whatever it was that he saw, it left him feeling wonderfully happy for many hours.

Now everything about his self-centred former life disgusted him. He couldn't possibly go back. It was the point of no return. Even the most vivid worldly dream that he'd had, that of entering into the service of a great lady – I don't know who she was – even that ultimate romantic and courtly sacrifice failed to stir him, as did the lives of the saints. He began to feel that he could be truly a great knight, but a different sort of knight, one who could equal the penances of those he was reading about; or perhaps he could bury himself in a Carthusian monastery, where nobody would ever hear of him again.

He had a vision of the Virgin Mary holding the baby Jesus, seemingly beckoning him to serve her. Mary seems to have an extraordinary power as an intermediary in the minds of those on the brink of conversion. In response, he had to do something dramatic, and that dramatic thing was going to be a pilgrimage to Jerusalem, something which was then an extraordinary thing to achieve. The few people who attempted it often died doing so. But the months were still passing and Inigo returned to the *Life of Christ.*, written by a Carthusian, Ludolph of Saxony.

Again, we would find it, no doubt, impossibly long and boring today, but for poor Inigo there was little alternative. Probably, Inigo read slowly. A knight like him wouldn't read every day as a matter of course. He may have read the words out aloud to himself. To pass the time he started a little exercise book, where he noted down the words of Christ in red, and the Virgin Mary in blue, and he would stop and ponder them, and meditate on passages that he read. For a religious person it all seems very natural nowadays, but one has to remember that religion was practised in a very different way in those days, and this was the beginning of what was to become a new form of meditation: reading the Gospel, and trying to live it in one's own mind. This is what Inigo was stumbling towards as he lay sick in that upstairs room in the Castle at Loyola.

He would imagine himself in the Gospel scene; be one of the participants; see it; listen to others and talk, himself, to the people there. This remains an extraordinarily vivid way of meditating – reading the Gospel every day and returning to it throughout the day as an actor in the drama.

He could not walk, but he could read slowly, and he could do what he would do for the rest of his life, which was simply to look at the stars, and to ponder the meaning of creation. If you go to the chapel now, at one end there is a statue of St Ignatius lying down, which tries to give an impression of his conversion experience. He has an exalted expression on his face, which is turned upwards.

Gradually as his strength returned he would go for short walks. His progress is marked to this day.

I sat there and heard the Mass (in Spanish of course) not understanding much at all, and slowly tried to work out how these two books, the only two in the Castle, had embedded themselves in Inigo's mind. The chapel is more of a room than a church but it has a powerful atmosphere.

Eventually, Inigo was well enough to begin his new life. His brother, Martin, was probably getting rather worried about Inigo's changed attitude. But, despite his unusual behaviour, Inigo was not yet prepared to admit to others that his whole life had changed, that he was going to give up his old life and go on a pilgrimage as a beggar and a hermit. That might have worried his brother even more. So he just admitted that he was off to see the Duke of Najera, without saying that his plan was really to break with his old life. He left the Castle and he was never to live there again.

Many religious people nowadays have had conversion experiences like Ignatius'; very few preserve a strong faith from childhood into maturity without a break. Such conversion experiences are often very sudden, as for example while attending a Billy Graham-type rally. Like Inigo's, it can be brought on by a sudden disaster, bereavement or change in one's life. For me, it was more gradual and is still incomplete.

I have already found that I am a religious person who has difficulty believing in God. In my twenties I was certainly not religious, but perhaps I always had a feeling for it. My mother used to take me to the local Catholic Church. As a teenager I would go on my own to the Brompton Oratory, where I had been confirmed. Then I gradually fell away. By the time I got married I hardly went to church at all. My wife would go and I would stay at home. Then I went to Lourdes and was inspired, but it all took a long time, years. In the heady delirium of sickness, Inigo was converted within weeks and he decided to give up everything – a resolution I have never remotely approached.

Meditation: Conversion

The Spirit of the Lord God is upon me... to give them a garland instead of ashes, the oil of gladness instead of mourning, the mantle of praise instead of a faint spirit. Isaiah 61:1 & 3.
I say to you, unless you turn and become like children, you will never enter the kingdom of heaven. Matthew: 18:3.
Do not marvel that I said to you, 'You must be born anew.' John 3:7.

Conversion experiences are sometimes mocked by the cynic. I have talked to priests who think that St Ignatius just decided to become a saint as he had decided to become a knight in shining armour. But his conversion was real. Maybe to be truly converted we have to renounce carping intellectualism, to become little children. For any parent the trusting faith of smaller children is truly touching. Can we renounce the intellect and trust to instinct or to authority as once before we trusted our parents?

We will never conquer our will by intellect. St Ignatius found joy in the reading of Scripture. He found irritation and lassitude in the reading of knightly tales. Instead of that half hour reading the newspaper designed to grab our attention and compare ourselves to celebrities rising and falling, why not read a Daily Missal for half an hour? Ignatian spirituality developed from Inigo's initial slow reading and visualisation of the Gospel passages.

Inigo's conversion was immediate, intense and all-encompassing. For most of us ours will not be like that. We will not give up our job, our family. We will remain as we are physically, but something will change within.

You might try this exercise. Go to the church in the morning and listen to the reading. Then try and remember it in the evening and you will be surprised how easy it is to muse on it. If God exists, should he be confined to the church? You don't speak to your partner in life only when you are in the house together.

Chapter 6
The Road to Manresa

Inigo's path lay to Aránzazu, a centre of pilgrimage in the Basque mountains. He spent a night there and probably made a vow of chastity before the shrine of Our Lady of Aránzazu. Then, it would have been a small mountain chapel at the head of a narrow path, which even a mule would have found difficult. This was the equivalent of a knight's vigil, but was, in this case, the start of a new life. Visiting his sister in Oñati, he made his way to Navarrette, to take his leave of the Duke of Nájera and his old life.

During the week that we were staying in Azpeitia, we too made a short pilgrimage to Aránzazu. One hot day we climbed aboard the people-carrier, made the usual stop at a supermarket where you can buy everything (which I think we did) and climbed up the winding mountain road. Now, the place is a vast shrine with a much admired – but hideous – modern church. Downstairs, in the crypt, is a chapel which approximates to the size of the old mountain chapel, surrounded by very modern, bright murals. Embedded in the church above is the tiny statue of Our Lady, which is the origin of all this. She is sitting crowned, holding the child Jesus who blesses us. There is a large car park and one can wander up a little lane to cafés and a restaurant, and on one's right, a huge gorge falls away to the deep valley below, and on one's left, there is a large hall where people can play Basque sports. It was all very ordinary.

I tried to ask a Franciscan monk more about the visit of St Ignatius but, like some of the other Spaniards I had met, I'm not sure he knew what I was talking about. He was a bit vague, and I had to make do with the guide book to describe the short visit. At the foot of the mountain we had lunch in Oñati, a small town with the atmosphere, at its centre, of an Oxford college. There is a medieval building with lawns and a river and a gatehouse, all on a small scale, but old and impressive with an academic feel. Here we sat on the grass and had our picnic. The children were none too impressed with the long drive up to Aránzazu, or with walking around it. Why should they share my enthusiasm? For them it was just another opportunity to play around and be naughty.

I piled them into the car and drove like a rocket down the mountain, all the way down to the sea where I could swim. It would have been very different for Inigo, plodding downwards with his mule, his wounded leg in agony, still dressed in nobleman's clothes, wondering what his life would bring in the future. He was still – no doubt, in a rather immature way – dreaming of imitating the lives of famous knightly saints who had given up everything. Inigo must now make the decisive break with his past.

The Duke gave Inigo some money that he was owed, and offered him a job, which he politely declined. He settled his debts, and started off on his road to Jerusalem. His plan was to make his way across Spain to Barcelona, where he could take a ship for Italy, and travel to Rome. There, he would ask the Pope for permission to make a pilgrimage to Jerusalem.

In those days everyone who wished to make a pilgrimage to Jerusalem had to ask permission, perhaps to avoid dangerous enthusiasms. He was to do all this long journey on foot, apart from the sea crossings. His road lay past Saragossa. Here a strange incident happened which he relates in his autobiography.

On the road he met a Moor, probably a Muslim, recently converted, perhaps forcibly, to Christianity. The Moor was prepared to accept the idea of a Virgin conception, but not of a Virgin Birth. Matters got heated and, after an aggressive exchange of words, the Moor rode off. Inigo felt his pride assaulted, and determined on stabbing the Moor with his dagger, but then his conscience afflicted him. He decided to leave matters to his mule. If the Moor took the road in one direction, he would follow him and kill him. If not, he would leave him alone. Despite the fact that the obvious route lay ahead of the Moor, the mule wisely took the other direction. Inigo had been saved from himself. How often does mere chance – or Providence under the guise of chance – change our lives? Inigo was at the crossroads between becoming a saint and a violent crusader.

He clearly had a long way to go if he could contemplate killing somebody just because of a religious argument. Before reaching Barcelona, he would visit Montserrat, a shrine which was already ancient. Montserrat means 'jagged mountain' and one can see from afar its serrated peaks rising high above the plain.

This shrine to Our Lady was already one of the most famous in Spain. Here, Inigo made a general confession lasting three days to a French monk, Jean Chanon. This wasn't the kind of rapid confession we tend to make, a few sins rattled off. Inigo spent three days preparing and meditating on all the sins of his very normal short life. For him this was indeed being born again. This was another decisive turning-point in his life. He spent a night in vigil before the shrine, took off his fine clothes, and gave them to a beggar, as well as donating his mule to the monastery. He had already bought a rough cloak and a scarf, and he now made his way down the hill to Manresa. He was overtaken by a constable who was worried that the beggar had perhaps stolen the clothes of the Hidalgo who had arrived a few days before.

Inigo was filled with remorse that he had caused trouble to the beggar, and he made his way down to the town where he probably only intended to spend a few days on his way to Barcelona, but where in fact he was to spend ten months.

Our own route to Montserrat was even more roundabout than that of Inigo. We had spent a week in the Hostel at Azpeitia and as it was August, there were no houses available to rent, so we decided to start making our way back home to England. We drove to a campsite in the Landes, where we spent a week on huge beaches filled with Germans who liked taking all their clothes off. The Landes coast is the modern world: a string of ugly new resorts inhabited by droves of tourists here to enjoy the delights of a seaside holiday. But nothing can detract from the beauty and power of the great seas that pound these wide beaches.

It was a nice compact campsite. We set up our three little tents amidst all the huge ones around about us, and splashed around in a swimming-pool. Then I suppose the idea was to start making our way back to London. But my conscience started to plague me. I hadn't really finished, in my view, my pilgrimage in the footsteps of St

Ignatius, so there was a terrible scene one day on the beach when I announced we were to go back to Spain. Of course, the children wanted to go back to England, to their friends and television. Eventually, after much protest, everyone agreed to go to Spain.

Once again, we stuffed everything, with great difficulty, back into the car and drove back across the Pyrenees, back down the motorway, through the town of Foix, where it started to pour with rain. The road to Manresa continued. We crept over the Pyrenees, asking along the way if we could stay, but of course, being summer, there was no room at any inn. Finally, late at night, we arrived at Manresa. I had looked it up in the Michelin guide the day before, and here we stayed, our only night in a smart hotel occupying two rooms, the children watching television.

We awoke the next morning to have breakfast looking out of the plate-glass windows at the river that I had come to see, the Cardoner. Ignatius, for the rest of his life, was to talk of the Cardoner experience.

Inigo had plodded along the road from Montserrat to Manresa – it is not far – and over the narrow Roman footbridge which is still there, to the town, which is not so different now from the way it was then. It still rises up the steep banks from the river, and it is still dominated by the Cathedral. On his way into the town he had met a lady, Ines Pascual, who with other ladies, was to help support him over the next ten months. It was at Manresa that Ignatius, as I think I might call him from now on, came to a degree of spiritual maturity.

From his first day there, he started to live a life of the utmost simplicity, begging in the street – how difficult that must have been for such a proud man, especially as people must have laughed at him; sleeping on the floor, and sitting alone in a narrow cave overlooking the River Cardoner. He had his little notebook in which to make observations – probably a little book of hours – thinking of St Dominic and St Francis, and trying to imitate their way of life. He hardly ate meat or drank wine, except perhaps on a Sunday, and he lived as much as possible on herbs, bread and very simple food, undergoing all sorts of penances and fasts, which were to leave him more or less ill for the rest of his life, suffering from severe stomach cramps.

The days passed. He did little except to pray a lot, and therefore he did much. At first he was very happy that he had made the decision to give up everything and live very simply, and then of course, doubts started appearing. These grew to such an extent that at one point he became almost suicidal, but he finally came through them, attaining a profound sense of peace. We can read his story as if he is living his own Exercises, his spiritual ups and downs and his reversals and breakthroughs, just as we experience a similar path.

He worried about whether he had really confessed his sins properly. At one stage, he even thought of throwing himself down a well that, for some reason, was in the middle of his room. He still went to Mass every day and Vespers in the evening but it was not enough. He began to stop eating, sometimes for a whole week. Eventually, he became very ill and might have died if he had not been made to wear proper clothes and look after himself by the religious ladies of the town who had adopted him. He was beset with scruples and his mood oscillated violently.

This change of mood was reflected later in his Spiritual Exercises, which shift from meditations on the joyful aspects of Christ's life to contemplations of his Passion. I think one of the reasons why the Spiritual Exercises are such a powerful tool is because our own mood can shift in this way. We can become beset by doubts. We can encounter a dark night of the soul when our prayers become arid and apparently unanswered. But often such a period leads to a profounder meditation on the saving grace of God, which in turn leads to a greater serenity and acceptance.

This is what seems to have happened to Ignatius. He realised he could not continue to be obsessed about what he regarded as his past sins. In effect he had to live for the present. We have to live for the present also. The past is gone into another world. It is irretrievable and can never be relived. This realisation of the certainty of the present moment is a powerful tool to peace and happiness. But Ignatius felt strongly too that his soul was fought over between good and evil, God and Satan, that only a profound acceptance of Jesus could save him, and that he had to be beside Christ at all times. Thus the only path to peace is to find God in all things and to worship him in all things.

It was after this dark period that he knew the serenity that was to stay with him for the rest of his life. It was also then that he started to work out what his vocation was. He began to jot down the notes that were to become The Spiritual Exercises: the foundation of his Movement, and his most famous book. He had let his hair and nails grow, and his appearance had become unkempt, but as the months passed he tidied himself up and had a new purpose in life. Visions of bright lights came to him.

Our time in Manresa was going to be much shorter than that of Ignatius. We made our way up to the huge

Jesuit church and buildings that dominate the side of the gorge where Ignatius had sat in his cave. While Mary was trying to deal with the children outside, a Jesuit priest befriended me and showed me around. Once inside the Baroque church, I sat in the tiny cave with its rough-hewn walls and ceiling where Ignatius had sat.

First though, we had to make our way to the local swimming-pool. It was a strange affair, right in the middle of the town, where I sat in the heat on the concrete, surrounded by modern buildings. I drove to Montserrat, now a vast place with a huge car park skirting the side of the mountain, with literally thousands of people wandering around. One can queue up at the side of the Basilica, climb the steps and touch the black Virgin of Montserrat, light a candle and do all the usual things. There are hotels there, cafés and a wonderful Vespers service. But it was getting late, so we made our way back down to the town where it was fiesta night, when everybody enjoys themselves, usually with some ancient religious festival as an excuse.

We had dinner at the little café where the singer, Famozo Pepe, entertained us. The song which the children seemed to love best was one which appeared to be made up entirely of English numbers one, two, three, four, five, six, seven, eight, nine, ten. Famozo obviously loved his job. He wanted everyone else to join in. Occasionally he would pluck people out of the crowd to join the singing and I shrivelled up in the corner hoping not to be picked out.

One night at the hotel was enough. We were very pleased that we had found a room in the youth hostel the next day. Unfortunately, it was right next to where an enormous band played in the street until 5.30 in the morning. Every hour or two it seemed to be coming to an end and then fired up again. At about 2am I packed my sleeping bag on my back and walked out of the town towards the gorge. I sat there looking at the stars, intending to go to sleep, but not being able to. It was quiet there and I tried to think about what this scene must have been like five centuries before, as I gazed over the ravine to Seto Cathedral.

Returning to the youth hostel at about 5am, I slept for a couple of hours and then went off to Mass in the chapel and said goodbye to the Jesuits. I packed my car and made my way to Barcelona. It was time now to leave Spain.

It is strange that such a small Spanish town, that most people have never heard of, had so profound an effect on Ignatius, on the history of the Jesuits, and therefore, on European history. There is nothing particularly startling about it, although the setting is majestic, but it was in this small town that I suppose Ignatius could come to terms with himself, with his simple round of begging in the streets, attending Mass, and starting to jot down his thoughts for The Spiritual Exercises. I now felt I would have to understand these very much better if I was to make any further progress in my quest for understanding St Ignatius. And this I was to do by visiting St Beuno's Retreat Centre in Wales a couple of months later.

Meditation: The road

You shall walk in all the way which the Lord your God has commanded you, that you may live. Deuteronomy 5:33.
Jesus said to him, "I am the way, and the truth, and the life; no one comes to the Father, but by me." John 14:6.

I am dubious of an instant life-changing conversion experience when thereafter everything is settled and perfect. For most of us the road is longer. And it is a road. Ignatius was still travelling, a spiritual road on his way to Manresa. His conversion up to now may have been shallow. In Manresa in solitude, both in the cave of the Spirit and in an actual cave, Ignatius grappled with and found a deeper spirituality.

We have to do the same. Every day will bring new challenges. What was settled and accepted yesterday will be thrown open to question in our minds tomorrow. The Manresa way of developing our spiritual life is one of the most effective – to be alone and take a text, any biblical text, and read it slowly again and again and visualise the scene. To live the Spirit in the world. The Spirit sustains and is a constant presence in the world.

We are constantly on a road, and it is the same with our spiritual life. Yet, with the Spirit, every day starts afresh. We can still find the Spirit in our final days. Some day we will know it in full, when released altogether from the present hard road. Now we can rest awhile and see it in glimpses, but see it we can, if we try.

You might attempt your own 'Manresa' experience. Go into a quiet place, read a short biblical text and think about what it means to you.

Chapter 7
Leaving Manresa

It was at Manresa that Ignatius made the first draft of the Spiritual Exercises. Until I had done a retreat myself based on the Exercises, this whole part of his life was difficult for me to understand; but it was Manresa which made Ignatius. It was here that, in writing the Spiritual Exercises, he finally and without any further doubt came to the conclusion that Christ had to be the centre of his life, and that Christ was the centre of the world, and of all history. He further realised that everything that had been and was to be, everything he had done and was to do, would be based on the life and the teachings of Christ.

So the little book that he wrote was simply what he thought would be a useful guide to people, so that they could come to understand what he considered to be essential truths. All that he did at Manresa during these months – the meditating in his cave; the begging on the streets; the marking up of his small exercise book in blue and red pen; all the long vigils that left his body so weak; cutting an ever larger hole in the sole of his shoe so that his feet became wet and uncomfortable; the various fasts that were to give him terrible stomach pains the rest of his life – all this was for one purpose: to put Christ at the centre of his life.

That time at Manresa for my family and me, of course, was so very different. We stayed there just two nights, one in a comfortable hotel, the next in a youth hostel. Our time was spent sitting in comfortable noisy cafes, looking after children, staying there as part of a holiday, but it had been in the same place. I looked at the same cathedral across the same Roman bridge spanning the same gorge, climbing the steep cobbled streets that Ignatius knew. When I walked through the town at four in the morning, when all was finally getting quiet after the fiesta, then some small echo of what Manresa had been like five centuries before came back and gave one an inkling. We left Manresa on a boiling hot day near the flowing Cardoner and drove along the motorway to Barcelona.

Ignatius was to stay there just twenty days. It was February 1523. His plan was now to visit Jerusalem and work there for the conversion of Muslims. But first he had to obtain the Pope's permission, and so he must take a ship from Barcelona to Italy. It was a relatively short walk to Barcelona. Whilst there, a lady called Isabel Roser saw his face light up as he was listening to a sermon. She seemed to hear a voice saying "Speak to him". She immediately recognised the special quality of his holiness and invited him home at the request of her husband. They looked after him and provided him with money (that he deliberately left behind on a bench) for his voyage, just taking on board a few hard biscuits. The trip of five days was to Gaeta on the Mediterranean coast of Italy, about sixty miles from Rome.

We drove ourselves to Barcelona, along the modern highway. Before we left, I asked at our youth hostel in Manresa if the youth hostel in Barcelona had room for us. "I don't know", said the girl at the reception desk. "Could you read for us the Spanish prospectus of the Barcelona youth hostel?" I asked. "They have space for five", she said. We were eight, all told, with the children. At this stage I remembered that I didn't even possess a youth hostel card. I had last gone hostelling thirty years before, hitch-hiking across Europe. The hostels were empty then. The girl now came back to us and said that the hostel in Barcelona was full. After all, it was spring. So we knew that there was going to be another sleepless night driving across Europe.

No doubt Ignatius had spent a day or two walking through Barcelona in 1523. I parked the car near the church where he worshipped, the Sacred Heart of Jesus. There, at a side altar, you can find a rather dusty glass case, ignored by everyone, containing the sword that Ignatius left behind at Montserrat. We were the only people that day looking at it. Moving into the city centre, we walked down the Rambla. There we saw a few 'human statues', which stand rock still until you drop a penny into their hat, then they do a little movement for you. There was a Pharaoh and his consort, and a devil, which frightened and grabbed Nicholas. We passed cages full of birds and tanks full of newts. The others walked back to get themselves a McDonald's. I walked towards the sea, in search of Ignatius' haunts in Barcelona.

I had a small pilgrim guide with which to search for the places. It was hot and tiring.

I made my way past the sea in search of the Basilica of Santa Maria del Mar, which had been Ignatius's parish church. He begged in one of its doorways. The guide told me that we are reminded of this by the tablet on the steps leading up to the door of the main nave. The church was locked, of course. One has to rise early or go late to find a church open in Spain. I walked all the way around, but found no tablet. I then walked up the street to look for Ines Pascual's house. It is no longer there. In its place is a seedy tenement. Ignatius was to live there on three occasions, on the way to Jerusalem, on his return to Barcelona and again later in his life. The house is on the corner of Princesca Street and the appropriately named St Ignatius Street. The atmosphere is still there. Narrow streets, lots of shade, heat and shutters – and, of course, noise.

I never found the home of Isabel Roser, the lady who came across him by chance at church. She fed and looked after him and had wanted to give him money for his voyage, which he refused. She wouldn't have known that he was making his way to Jerusalem. In those days, a pilgrimage to Jerusalem was altogether too dangerous a thing. Many people assumed that the pilgrims would never come back, and Ignatius would have been concerned that people might think he was trying to make himself a martyr, or simply showing off. As it was, his friends still begged him to take a companion, on the grounds that he knew no Latin or Italian and would find it hard to make his way in Rome. But he decided to go alone, because he wanted to prove to himself that he had to rely only on God.

Having found his haunts, I wandered slowly back to the car and bought myself a Coke. We finally found a bar where we could have a snack. That evening we left Barcelona and Spain. Our holiday was coming to an end, and we drove back across southern France to stay with an aunt in Switzerland, and then back home. My footsteps in search of Ignatius in Rome would have to wait until next year.

Meditation: Leaving

Entreat me not to leave you or to return from following you; for where you go I will go. Ruth 1:16.
Where I am going you cannot follow me now; but you shall follow afterward. John 13:36.

I hate leaving anywhere, returning to London from Lincolnshire, for example. But arriving is easier. We all worry about leaving, letting go, and the greatest fear we have is of leaving life. But dying must be like falling asleep. We don't fear falling asleep because we know we cannot stop ourselves; sooner rather than later it is inevitable. It is pleasurable and we know we must wake.

Can we have such faith that we will wake from dying? We cannot. But dying itself cannot be difficult. We never remember exactly how or when we fell asleep. When we wake from death, it will, I suppose, be the same.

You might also try a "leaving" exercise. Does leaving anything or anywhere for a few days make you slightly depressed? Try linking the experience to a Gospel reading and see if it gives you more hope in renewal through change.

Chapter 8
Rome

Nowadays a trip of seventy miles or so from Gaeta to Rome would be an easy one that you could drive in a couple of hours. But for Ignatius, it was long and hazardous. Of course, he walked there, and it would have taken him several days; but that wasn't the real problem. He joined up with a couple of travelling companions, a lady and her daughter, and there was an incident where some drunken soldiers tried to rape them. Ignatius had to protect his travelling companions and chase the soldiers away. On another occasion, perhaps at Fondi, the small party were locked out of a town altogether because of the plague. It seems to be a constant refrain of Ignatius' travels around Italy that the plague was raging intermittently, and that he was locked out of towns and thrown into ditches because of fear that travellers spread the plague. Generally malnourished as he was, he suffered quite extraordinary tribulations for such an easy journey.

In any event, he had arrived in Rome by Palm Sunday, in March 1523. There was no difficulty in obtaining permission from the Pope, Adrian VI, to go to Jerusalem. Naturally, once again, there was also no shortage of people who tried to dissuade him from making such a perilous journey. I don't know where he stayed, perhaps in the Spanish hospice, near the Piazza Navona.

He was now to start his long journey to Jerusalem, but first of all he had to walk half the length of Italy, from Rome to Venice and across the Apennines on foot and on short rations. After obtaining permission from Adrian VI, he was given a special Certificate. It can still be seen in the Vatican archives, written in Latin: *"Ignatius of Loyola from the Diocese of Pamplona, is given permission to go on pilgrimage to the Holy Land, March 21, 1523."*

The walk from Rome to Venice is the best part of four hundred miles, a long way for a man with a limp, whose legs had been so badly smashed up the year before. His friends had given him some money (seven crowns) but it was altogether too easy just to live off the money, so he promptly gave it away to a beggar and made his way himself as a beggar, living from hand to mouth. He was alone, without the normal companionship of a pilgrim group to talk, laugh and sing with. Then, as now, pilgrimages were as much social events as they were religious ones, but none of this was for Ignatius. He walked alone.

Once again, towns were closed due to the plague. At Chioggia he received a vision of Christ, and the next day was able to enter Venice despite not having a Certificate against Plague. Entering a city without such a Certificate was a dangerous and difficult thing to do, but somehow Ignatius managed it. He had nowhere to stay and wouldn't ask for hospitality from anyone, so he just lay down on a stone bench outside the Doge's Palace. (The Doge being the elected head of the then Republic of Venice). There he was befriended, I don't know why, by a Spaniard who ranked high in the service of Venice. This man introduced him to the Doge and other colleagues, and arranged a passage for him – a very dangerous passage, down the Adriatic to Cyprus and then from Cyprus to the Holy Land.

People were getting alarmed at Ignatius' dishevelled appearance and sickly pallor, and they advised him once again not to proceed. He was told that if he did go to sea he would probably be buried there, but naturally he insisted on going ahead, and he survived the journey. There was even a risk that he might be thrown overboard by some sailors who resented all his advice to them to live a better life, but he survived this threat too.

The visit I and my family made to Venice was rather different. This was not to be the first stop on a hazardous pilgrimage to fight the Turks, but the last part of a family holiday. You could say we slummed it a little. The children helped set up our tents on the sand of the Marina de Venezia along with, it seemed, thousands of German tourists, from where we made daily excursions by boat across to Venice. No doubt we passed through many of the sites that Ignatius had passed through five centuries before, and if he were alive today he would probably have very little difficulty in recognising the city and its transport as being much the same that he enjoyed.

Like him, we wandered through St Mark's Square and past the Doge's Palace – unlike him, with our pushchair. Nor did we have to sleep on the stone benches, which are still there. Like him, we sat down in or wandered through all the churches, not in some state of religious fervour, but trying to persuade the children not to make too much noise, and perhaps getting them to light a candle before promising them another ice cream or visit to a café.

One church I visited was the Gesuiti, the eighteenth-century Jesuit church of Venice. Who would have thought that this wandering beggar, ignored by the crowds as he sat on the porches of churches and begged some miserable few pennies which he promptly gave to other beggars, this man whom everybody ignored, would, just over one and a half centuries after his death, inspire the creation of this Baroque splendour? But, in spite of the simplicity of his own life, Ignatius would not have disapproved. While poverty was his calling, nothing, in his view, was too rich for God. In the Baroque period his Order was keen to glorify God to the maximum through magnificent architecture, art and church furnishings.

Like Ignatius at the time of his visit, and like countless thousands of others before and since, we left no mark on this city. Ignatius himself tells us absolutely nothing about it. He visited Venice in its moment of greatness. He was introduced to the great Doge Andrea Gritti, whose features, under his strange hat, we can still gaze at in a myriad of reproductions. I can only gaze at the likeness, but Ignatius talked to the man; the man who was then one of the arbiters of Europe, the republican leader of a great power. At this time Venice was the Great Republic, and thanks to that meeting, Ignatius received free passage to Cyprus.

Meditation: God and Google

The Lord stood by him and said, 'Take courage, for as you have testified about me at Jerusalem, so you must bear witness also at Rome' Acts 23:11.

A friend of mine is dying of cancer. Waking in the night I tried to concentrate on him, praying for him. I found it comforting and pleasant to pray for someone else for a change; somebody not myself, not close to me. We are happiest when doing things for other people.

So many millions of pilgrims come to Rome every year, and likewise tourists to Venice, that, among the swarming crowds, I wondered, as I often do, how God can listen to all our prayers? There are so many billions of us. I ran this thought past a priest and a deeply religious friend of mine. The priest said that God is effectively different parts in one. This makes sense if we acknowledge the Trinity, the three-in-one.

God may not be so much an old man with a beard as an essence of unlimited parts; but he must also have a single will and intelligence, otherwise he is some amorphous New Age creature, a god who is reduced to the level of equality with his own creation – a classic case of neo-pantheism, or nature-worship.

My friend told me that when you perform a search in *Google,* your message goes to one of 450,000 linked computers in America. So *Google,* like God, can listen to millions of people at once, while still being a single entity! Does this answer my question of how God can exist as a listener to prayers? Insofar as any analogy with man-made structures can, it may do.

This difficult thought leads me to try to solve another thought. I have long believed that we are too focused on ourselves as individuals. Heaven must be being part of the unity of everything that has been and will be. It is an eternal, joyous, overwhelming gasp of wonder at reunification with God, with everything, but this leads me to another difficulty.

If prayer means anything, our petitions should be able to change things. But, if as a result of prayer we change even one thing, doesn't that have a myriad of consequences that have to start changing everything else? Furthermore, if billions of people are doing this, how can complete chaos be avoided, with parallel histories and events competing with each other? For that reason, we know it is impossible to go back in time, because the very fact of going back would change the present, but if in heaven we see everything now, in the past and in the future, isn't there a single time-line? Do these worries matter?

You might try thinking about this problem. Put yourself in the position of God for a moment. How would you cope with all these requests? Perhaps we should think of him a bit more. Ask a little less and give a little more.

Chapter 9
Jerusalem and the Journey Home

Luckily for Ignatius, his pilgrim ship made good enough time for him to avoid the fate of being thrown overboard to appease the gods, and also saved his fellow passengers from his sermonising. He and his fellow pilgrims had to travel across Cyprus, from Famagusta to Larnica, where they caught up with the first pilgrim ship from Venice. Ignatius was once again allowed on the boat for free and he arrived safely in Jaffa. After a journey of forty eight days, the pilgrims walked the last few miles into Jerusalem. At last they had arrived at their destination.

They were shown the holy places, including the Holy Sepulchre (the tomb of Christ), and they travelled on to Bethlehem. However, Ignatius was not interested in behaving like other pilgrims, acting like a sightseer and doing what he was told. For him, the visit wasn't an end in itself, it was going to be the beginning, as far as he was concerned, of a lifetime's work.

He wanted to stay in Jerusalem to convert the unbelievers. No doubt there was already lurking in his mind some impractical notion of founding a new Order which would achieve great things. But he was soon brought down to earth by the Franciscan Superior who was responsible for looking after Christians under Turkish rule. He refused to let him do such work, and threatened him with excommunication if he did so.

The Christian community was too poor either to maintain or ransom him if he was caught by a band of Islamic extremists who, at that time, were rampaging through Jerusalem. Ignatius accepted the ruling. He did, however, slip away from his guardians to pay one last visit to the Mount of Olives, to the spot where he looked for the imprint on the rock from which Jesus had ascended to heaven. He had to give away his last pen-knife, one of the few possessions remaining with him, to see the spot. But, as far as he was concerned, it was well worth it, despite the danger of being hit on the head with a stick by his guardian, once his unauthorised absence was noted.

I didn't visit Jerusalem on pilgrimage myself, but as part of an official trip. Therefore, the feelings were not as elated as they would have been in the case of a pilgrim who had travelled forty-eight days to reach it, rather than a few hours on a comfortable flight. However jaded one is, no one ever forgets their first visit. The breathtaking view from the Mount of Olives today, over the city to the Dome of the Rock, is the same as Ignatius saw that night as he dodged his guards. The atmosphere of religious tension is still the same. The Holy Sepulchre is still a mass of competing chapels from every Christian church, as it was in his day. One walks down the same narrow streets and while, of course, there is no comparison now with the way that tourists used to be treated, as a Christian one cannot help but feel a slight sense of unease, as an interloper into what is primarily a Jewish and Muslim city.

Like Ignatius, we too want to pursue our religious Jerusalem, but sometimes it is others who decide our route. Ignatius might have been an unknown Franciscan cocooned in a Muslim city for the rest of his life. Fate, or divine providence as Ignatius would no doubt have put it, had other ideas.

When Ignatius and his fellow pilgrims arrived at Jaffa, there were three ships available. Ignatius was forced to take the smallest and most leaky vessel. The owners of the other two wanted payment and, as chance would have it, the smallest boat was the only one to survive the journey – the other two were shipwrecked. Ignatius arrived safely back in Venice. What was he now to do with the rest of his life? He was humble enough to appreciate that his ideas were half-baked, that he would have to go back to the drawing board. He must learn his new trade as a man of God and take a degree in theology. He was thirty-two.

So, he started the journey back to Barcelona, through a northern Italy ravaged by war. On one occasion he was arrested as a spy and regained his freedom only by acting as a mentally-ill person. A week later he was captured by a party of French soldiers. Their captain asked him where he was from, and upon hearing Ignatius' reply that he was from Guipuzcoa, the captain said "I come from near there, for it seems it is near Bayonne". His captor, a fellow Basque, ordered that he be well treated and fed. Even his trip across the sea was eventful, because his ship was among those pursued by the Genoese admiral Andrea Doria.

Perhaps the most important part of Ignatius's journey home was the memories it left him with. Despite his trials and tribulations, poverty, near shipwreck, arrest as a spy, he came through them all not despite, but because of, his insouciance. There is a verse in Italian that sums up his attitude:

Se tu segue tua stella, non puoi fallire a glorioso porto.

Or, if you follow your star, you cannot fail to reach a glorious haven.

It had been an exciting trip, but, a year after he had left he was back in Barcelona, safe and sound. His career as a missionary pilgrim was over for the time being, and many years of study and hard work now opened up before him.

What was he to do with his life? He just wanted others to find God as he had found him.

Meditation: Jerusalem and home

You have come to Mount Zion and to the city of the living God, the heavenly Jerusalem. Hebrews 12:22.
Wise men from the East came to Jerusalem. Matthew 2:1.

My mind was flitting from one subject to another. I didn't try to concoct a meditation based on Jerusalem, but every time my thoughts raced ahead too wildly, I just said "Jerusalem" to myself. I found it strangely comforting. Sometimes, even, thoughts on Jerusalem started acquiring a theme: its history, the conflict between Arab and Jew, the Crusades, the passion of Jesus going up to Golgotha.

As I deliberately returned my thoughts to Jerusalem on a hill, a Mount Sion – I sensed peaceful symbolism, a powerful physical and spiritual presence. A centre of all things. Again, my thoughts quietened. I awoke a couple of times in the night and, as my thoughts started to move ahead too fast, I returned to saying "Jerusalem" quietly, and sleep gently overcame me.

Try this, or any word that brings you peace – "Jesus", "Mary". Repeat it slowly. Live just for that word in that instant.

Think about a place in the Bible: Jerusalem will do. Imagine yourself there, walking around, seeing things, commenting. Put yourself there at different moments in history.

Pray let your servant return, that I may die in my own city, near the grave of my father and my mother. 2 Samuel 19:37.
No city or house divided against itself will stand. Matthew 12:25.

It had been a bad morning, A tube train delayed on the way to the dentist to have my gums cleaned and hacked at, a hastily summoned taxi. Another tube to catch a train at the station, followed by a wrong connection and another taxi. I got the taxi to let me off at the edge of Market Rasen, in Lincolnshire.

I sat at the back of the Victorian Catholic church. Immediately I felt happy. All my questions and lack of answers about God faded away. Later I started walking back home over the Lincolnshire wolds. I knew why I felt happy – I do not need a vocation to live the religious life in a monastery or to be ordained a deacon.

What gives me happiness, I think, is the Real Presence, on the altar, of the Blessed Sacrament. That is the mystery and power that I felt at the back of that church. How strange that this truth for me had only dawned on the evening of a long boring day. I hadn't really meant to be there. I had wanted to be at Downside, but if I had sat for two days at the monastery, maybe I wouldn't have had this insight.

You might find all this to be a bit strong a brew for you. I am not asking you to believe in the Real Presence, in other words that God is actually there in the church. I just want to give it to you as a thought that might help you. Do just try sitting in the back of any church. You don't have to attend a service. Incidentally, that is why it is so important to keep churches unlocked.

Chapter 10
Barcelona

Ignatius was now back at square one and he settled down to learn Latin grammar. He realised he wouldn't get anywhere without an education. By now all his Latin from school, twenty years ago, would have been forgotten. He sat amongst schoolboys, showing a fair amount of humility in being prepared to do so. He was lodged in the attic of his friend, Ines Pascual, although he refused her offer of a comfortable bed, preferring to lie on the floor. He made his living by begging, but gave most of it away.

Gradually his reputation for saintliness increased, and a small band of companions gathered around him, but he had his enemies as well. There was a convent whose well-bred nuns, not uncommonly in those days, had become so lax in their observances that young men used to frequent it – no doubt for reasons other than talking about God. When Ignatius tried to bring the nuns back to the straight and narrow, he was beaten up to within an inch of his life and had to spend a month in bed. After two years of studying, his tutor, Jeronimo Ardevol, deemed him ready to enter university and he made his way to Alcalá.

All this time he continued his mortifications: wearing a hair shirt; cutting holes in the soles of his inadequate shoes; eating badly – or barely at all – and praying half the night. People later recounted that such was his fervour that, at times, he was even raised supernaturally from the ground. In the canonisation proceedings after his death there was even a hint that Ignatius had managed to bring back to life a would-be suicide. This man had hanged himself and was lying insensible in the street for long enough for people to think him dead; but perhaps the incident became embellished as his reputation grew.

One might think people's memories had become over-excited as a result of his later reputation, yet such claims, often in the form of sworn testimony, have been made frequently about many saints, including Ignatius' great contemporary religious founders Teresa of Avila and Philip Neri (who was a friend).

Alcalá

Ignatius then made his way to Alcalá to continue his studies. Life would have been easy if he had acted as a normal student and confined himself to a little learning. Of course, he didn't. He was followed by three of his companions and was soon joined by a fourth. They dressed alike in grey.

Ignatius stirred up controversy by going every week to Communion, something that was then very rare, by visiting the sick and the poor and by preaching. He wasn't helped by some of his over-enthusiastic followers. Under his influence a woman and her two daughters were making a pilgrimage barefoot and begging. There was a real problem at this time with wandering bands of the *illuminati*, and the authorities were particularly sensitive to heresy from people who were pseudo-mystics or Gnostics. The *illuminati* were a Gnostic sect claiming special powers for themselves that allowed them to do pretty well what they wanted. Like many "charismatics", they resented any authority other than their own and were therefore considered a danger to the existing religious establishment. In an age when everybody was at least outwardly religious, these matters were held to be immensely important. The authorities therefore were closely concerned in monitoring all religious activities and their potential threat to good order in the state.

Ignatius was locked up and interrogated by the Archbishop's representative, because of suspicions that he was one of the *illuminati*. Conditions were imposed on his study, which amounted to him being required to act like any other, and his followers had to wear ordinary clothes.

Although Alcalá was a recent foundation, it was acquiring a reputation across Europe, thanks to the fame of its founder, Cardinal Cisneros. Ignatius was probably too busy meeting people to study properly, and he was ordered to go back to his books. It was time for him and his disciples to move on to a freer atmosphere at Salamanca.

Salamanca

Ignatius had only been a few days at Salamanca when he was again in trouble with the Inquisition. Thinking that he was just going to Confession, he was closely questioned and locked up in a filthy prison with his friends. Once again, he was told he must study quietly for four years, but Ignatius was not prepared to accept these conditions. There was only one solution. He must make his way to the greatest university of all, where he would be free – Paris. Retracing his steps and undertaking a hazardous journey on foot of over seven hundred miles when France and Spain were at war, he arrived in Paris in February 1528.

It has sometimes been said that Ignatius was the first hippie wandering around Europe doing his own thing (though such a description betrays great ignorance both of the saint's profoundly un-hippie-like mortifications and of the fact that he was trying not to do "his own thing" but God's will). Nowadays we are used to the modern craze for travelling, particularly by the young. Then, it was very unusual.

I first went to Spain myself as a student, hitch-hiking across that vast country when I was eighteen – it is a long time ago now and my memory of it is hazy. I can't pretend that I had any religious sensibilities or views whatsoever, and my trip had no particular purpose in mind, I wasn't studying. I was simply wandering across Europe, making for Lisbon where my grandfather lived.

I have memories of university towns, of kindness, of heat, and of great distances. It is an extraordinary thought that, whereas I was getting lifts in lorries and had some money on me, Ignatius was actually walking across this huge country and, walking with a limp as a wounded war veteran, without any resources whatsoever except what he could beg at the end of each day. He must have needed heroic courage and resilience, as well as a willingness to throw himself absolutely on God's providence. Very few of us are prepared to do that.

As a student, I stayed in spartan, but perfectly comfortable, youth hostels. I had my little guide books and maps, always making for somewhere to stay for the night. Ignatius had no such worries. He just lay down on any old floor of a friend or well-wisher, and his very willingness not to worry about himself gave him a sense of freedom which is denied to most people. Only he who has no sense of possession is completely free. Ignatius was one such person.

Paris

Enrolled at the university, then the greatest in the world, with some 4,000 students in a city of 300,000 souls, Ignatius soon suffered a setback. What little money he had from his friends in Paris he lent to another friend, who promptly squandered it. He was forced to move to cheaper lodgings, but the daily courses, from 5am to 7pm, were so long, and his lodgings so far away that he did not have the time to study and to beg in order to live. He was forced to go on fund-raising trips to Flanders and even London to raise money from the Spanish merchant community.

About this time, Ignatius became acquainted with what was to become his favourite book – *The Imitation of Christ,* by Thomas à Kempis (d.1471), still popular today, and also my favourite. One can see why it appealed to Ignatius. It is fundamentally about the renunciation of the world. Ignatius realised that celibacy and virtue could not be successfully imposed from outside by any set of rules, they had to come from within.

About this time too he began to give, for the first time, his full thirty-day retreat. The effect on three Spanish tutors at the university was dramatic. It changed their lives, in the same way they have had a profound effect on many, if not most, of those who have attempted them. These tutors felt that, from now on, anything secular was only of nominal importance to them. They had to devote their lives to God.

Already rumours about Ignatius' charisma were spreading. At this time, he asked the Inquisition to give him a clean bill of health. It was typical of the man that he requested a written statement of his orthodoxy, bearing the seal of the Inquisition, so that he could produce it for inspection in case he was ever suspected of heresy in the future.

While set upon his studies, it was time for him to acquire his first permanent companion. His early Spanish ones had not been able to follow him to Paris.

Meditation: Studies

I meditate on all that thou hast done; I muse on what thy hands have wrought. Psalm 143:5.
The beginning of wisdom is this: Get wisdom. Proverbs 4:7.
Do your best to present yourself to God as one approved. 2 Timothy 2:15.

We devote so much of our life to studies. We need to reach an elementary level even to have a job. But how important are they? Can we learn to be content with our modest abilities?

As I walked out of Market Rasen towards the Wolds, I passed the small hill where, some four hundred and seventy years before, the Pilgrimage of Grace had gathered in Lincolnshire. They were in rebellion against Henry VIII over the abolition of their traditions and Latin Mass. Their leaders went to a grisly fate, hung in cages and executed brutally; the Vicar of Louth hanged from his own steeple.

I am no partisan in this. There were cruelties on both sides, but it occurred to me, after that long morning in the train and the brief encounter with the Blessed Sacrament in the church, how lucky I was. Not particularly clever or successful but, while many people feel barely touched when they are in a church, when I enter one I feel this great sense of contentment.

However, I don't believe that is a gift given to some and not to others. In time, this capacity builds unknowingly if we work at it.

This great gift of the presence of God is waiting inside all of us. If you too, open your mind, whether in church or anywhere else, I think you will find that something moves within you.

Chapter 11
Companions

It was in Paris that Ignatius began to gather those who would be his permanent friends, lifelong companions, and joint founders of his new Society.

Francis Xavier, the future missionary *par excellence,* like him a nobleman from Navarre in Spain and a good sportsman; the popular Peter Favre, from a modest background in the French Alps, already a priest, and hugely intelligent; Diego Laynez, a future General of the Order; Alfonso Salmeron, whom he had known at Alcalá; Simón Rodriguez, who was to found the Society of Jesus in Portugal; and Nicholas Bobadilla, also from Spain. With all of them, Ignatius used his little book of Exercises to change their lives.

Sometimes, his friends would fast severely for days, meditate, and cut themselves off from the world. Gradually, a joint resolution took root, they would go off together to the Holy Land and, if necessary, die there.

Meanwhile, around them raged the argument that was to lead to their true vocation. The Calvinist doctrine of 'justification by faith alone' (a development of Luther's doctrine) was sweeping through Paris. This teaching denied that any good work could contribute to salvation; denied, in fact, that men had any free will at all. According to Calvin, God simply predestined most to hell and a select few, 'the Elect', to heaven, and there was nothing anyone could do to change that. There were savage Inquisitions. Ignatius himself was again questioned, but he persevered in his work. All the time, indeed, he carried on with his academic work, receiving first his BA, then in March 1535 his MA.

With Europe under threat from the Turks, it might indeed have seemed that the new Society would concentrate its work in the East. In fact, a large part of it would be nearer at hand. On finishing their degrees, the companions vowed to travel together to the Holy Land to preach to and convert Muslims and, if this proved impossible, to place themselves under the orders of the Pope. On the Feast of the Assumption, August 15 1534, they made their way to the Chapel of the Martyrs, in a crypt below what was then the church of St Denis, Montmartre. Favre said Mass and they made their vows.

In some parts of Europe, Ignatius has left a heavy footprint. If you travel to Loyola in the Basque country, his presence is everywhere, but in most places, of course, there is no sign and no recollection. In Barcelona, if you have the energy, you can search for a few plaques placed on the side of buildings. In Pamplona too, you will find one or two references; but when you come to Paris, all is extinguished.

You can only, I suppose, get some small idea of his life by visiting, as I have done so many times, my favourite part of Paris: the Left Bank student quarter. There you get a faint echo of the generations of foreign students who have come to this great university over the centuries – but how different the atmosphere would have been in the sixteenth century! It would have been much more like a spartan English public school of the early part of the nineteenth century than a modern, cosmopolitan, free-wheeling university. In the churches of Notre Dame and Saint Germain des Prés, within sights and sounds — or certainly within walking distance — of the Seine, you can sit or kneel where once Ignatius knelt. In a Gothic archway here, a strip of green there, the remains of some ancient house, some dim reflection reaches one of life five centuries ago. Though what one can never experience is the atmosphere of fervid religious controversy which raged in these streets and permeated every aspect of life.

Meditation: Companions

Woe to him who is alone when he falls and has not another to lift him up. Ecclesiastes 4:10.
Other boats were with him. Mark 4:36.
The right hand of fellowship. Galatians 2:9.

I walked, tired, into the small Alpine chapel at Ormarets at dusk and sat before the Blessed Sacrament, before walking back down the steep hill to home. That night I dreamt I was trying to set up some political organisation or other, I don't remember what, but it went wrong. The organisation, being political, was an unfriendly and bitter place. Where was true friendship?

I woke and thought that I was due to meet the Cardinal. One idea I would like to put to him is this: I believe there should be a meeting every week, or at least starting with once a month in the Cathedral. It should be for those struggling with unbelief. It should proclaim the value, not of instant conversion, but steady prayer – Mass-going, praying the Divine Office, expecting no miracles, not suddenly being blessed with unquestioning faith but with companions.

How joyous such a little meeting would be! It doesn't need a priest, we would give each other strength. There are times when we need no structures or organisations. We need to meet and talk, and listen.

You will find it very difficult to make progress on your own. Sooner or later you're going to have to take the plunge and join some sort of prayer group, where you can be helped along by the experience of others.

Chapter 12
Return to Spain

As a result of all the penances, most of them severe and, one might think, unnecessary, that Ignatius had forced upon himself in Manresa, his health had worsened once more. Now he was advised that only some fresh home air would do him any good (this was very common medical advice in those days). Perhaps we too need occasionally to return to our roots to take stock and start again.

Once more he made the long journey back home on foot, with only a donkey for companionship. Arriving in Azpeitia, he was met by his brother's servants who had heard of his arrival, but he refused all offers of hospitality and accommodation in the family home. Indeed, once he started on his life as a pilgrim, he was never to stay in the family home again. He insisted on living nearby, in a cheap, mean hostel in the village.

During this short time in his home town he sought to reform local practices, help the needy, and get the able-bodied poor back to work. His own condition, however, did not improve. Indeed, his colic was so bad that it was thought he might die, but he did not. However, his simple sermons did increasingly have an effect. He preached simply about the need to give up sin. People were not used to priests talking to them in the streets in their own language in this way. He started to change things in a small way, for instance in having bells rung regularly.

He made his way via Pamplona to Valencia to visit the families of his new Society and inform them that they had renounced the world. During this trip he visited an old friend, now the governess of the future Philip II, who was to see him and remember him years later. It was fourteen years since he had last been in Pamplona, when he had been so horribly wounded. It must have seemed to him that he had achieved very little in that time.

How many of us feel the same way! All he had done was to be a student and undertake a botched pilgrimage to Jerusalem. But, after seeming failure, the seeds of something great had been planted. Who would have thought that this ragamuffin, mature student was about to create one of the most influential Religious Orders in history? The fact is so well-known to us that it seems a cliché, but, with God's help, we too must have faith in ourselves. Out of small beginnings and against impossible odds, something great can be achieved.

Ignatius was now making his way back to Italy. At sea, the ship was rocked by a great storm and the other passengers started to panic. Ignatius quietly examined his conscience and wished he could have achieved more, as so many of us do when we finally come face to face with our end. He said later, "I prepared myself for death by examining my conscience, the thought of my sins." But yet again, this was not to be the end of Ignatius. There was still work to do. The ship weathered the storm and he arrived safely at port in Italy. He was never to leave it again.

Meditation: Return

Return, O my soul, to your rest; for the Lord has dealt bountifully with you. Psalm 116:7.
Jesus returned in the power of the Spirit into Galilee. Luke 4:14.

The next night I dreamt again. I was meeting the Cardinal again. I was putting to him my thought that too many Catholic priests seem reluctant to argue with people's lack of belief. Young people are put off initially by the seeming certainty of the belief of priests. It is a 'them and us' situation.

So, in my dreamlike conversation with the Cardinal, I suggested a regular meeting that could focus on people's struggle with belief, but which would be realistic about how that struggle could be resolved. We accept many things we cannot prove in life. Faith must be one of them.

Do you also find it irritating that, when you go to church, the priest or minister assumes you are a believer? You could consider going up to him or her afterwards and ask for a "formation", explaining and justifying belief.

Chapter 13
Italy – The Society is Founded

As was his custom, incredibly, Ignatius walked from Genoa to Venice. At one point, the path became so narrow and high by the side of a gorge that he could neither turn back nor go forward without great risk. He crept up the side of a high ravine and eventually made it to safety. At another point, he fell into a gutter and arrived in town dripping and dirty, with people laughing at him.

Arriving in Venice in 1536, he started to give The Spiritual Exercises, notably to Diego de Hoces, who was to become one of his first companions to die. Ignatius wrote letters and raised money for his friends to join him from Paris. As usual, he met with criticism. In Venice, he came across for the first time the future Cardinal and Pope Carafa who, with Gaetano di Thiene (St Cajetan) and two others, had founded the Theatines, an Order with some similarities to the yet-to-be-founded Jesuits. Ignatius was critical of the Theatine rule, which he thought too strict. He correctly saw that his new Order had to avoid spending time singing in choir, and should instead concentrate on going out and meeting people.

Sermons at Mass and regular Communion had become rare by the sixteenth century. Preaching in the open air to crowds was non-existent, but the reversal of all this was in the future. The idea of preaching and teaching to the local people grew slowly, as if by chance. At this stage, Ignatius and his friends still wanted to go to the Middle East.

The first companions arrived from France in early 1537, having made their way on foot from Paris, a distance of over six hundred miles, arguing with Protestants on the way. Nine had come from Paris. Ignatius had three new friends from Venice, the newcomers were Paschase Broët, Claude Le Jay, both priests, and Jean Codure, all from France. The group was still very small. They started to work in local hospitals.

The group left for Rome, to obtain the Pope's blessing for their trip to Jerusalem, but Ignatius decided to stay behind. Being an Italian, Carafa, now a Cardinal, disliked the invading Spaniards on principle, and Ignatius decided, wisely, to keep a low profile. The companions had the usual harsh journey, begging on the way, suffering bed lice and bad weather. Pope Paul III received them enthusiastically and gave them permission to be ordained. Finally, back in Venice, on 24 June 1537, Ignatius and his companions were ordained. Now all were priests.

The long-awaited moment of travelling to Jerusalem was going to have to be put off. War was once more raging with Turkey. There would be no pilgrim ships that year of the type Ignatius had taken fourteen years earlier. The companions decided to disperse around the local area and wait twelve months. If it was still not possible to travel to Jerusalem, they would put themselves at the disposal of the Pope. They decided they would call themselves the 'Companions of Jesus'. During this period, as at Manresa, Ignatius was often tempted to become a hermit, retiring from the world altogether, but he knew this was a temptation. His work lay in the world.

Exonerated one more time by the Inquisition, he set out for Rome. On the way, at a small place called La Storta, he had a vision of God the Father associating him with His Son, who spoke the words *"Ego vobis Romae propitius ero"* – I shall be favourable to you in Rome. Ignatius had no idea what it meant. He heard Christ saying again, "I want you to serve me." Ignatius was deeply overjoyed. When I read this passage about Ignatius' life for the first time, I too felt a great joy in my heart.

Ignatius now felt confident that he was on the right path. In Rome, he gave his Exercises to the great diplomat and would-be Church reformer Cardinal Contarini, who was enraptured by them, and was to be a great supporter. Ignatius and his companions would need this support in Rome, as they were soon to be attacked again, this time by a friar, who accused them of being "closet Lutherans".

The companions – still only a handful of them – were now gathering in Rome. From their modest home near the Ponte Sisto, they went out to preach. They surprised the city with their strange new commitment to public speaking in the squares and streets, speaking in a strange mixture of Latin and bad Italian. However, what they lacked in linguistic skill, was made up for in their faith and conviction. Every day they got up very early to say Mass, at separate altars, as was the norm before the days of concelebration, and they ate together in the evening. When a great famine hit the city, the companions impressed everyone with their commitment to the poor; begging themselves, they gave away their scanty alms to those in more need than themselves.

At the end of 1538 Ignatius said his first Mass. Perhaps he had delayed so long because he had wanted to say it in Jerusalem. It was eighteen months after his ordination! Not knowing that his brother Martin had died two months before, he wrote to him on 15 February, 1539. "I have gone at Christmas to St Mary Major's and there have said, by the help and grace of God, my first Mass in the chapel which contains the crib in which the infant Jesus was laid." Following his ordination, he had spent forty days in retreat and silent prayer. He found this a great consolation. It was a new Manresa for him.

The companions now had to decide whether to form a proper Society, with a Superior. Before this, they had intended themselves just to be a loose grouping directly under the orders of the Pope. But after long discussions, they decided to set up a Society which would go on existing after their deaths. But first they had to overcome the objections of a Commission headed by Cardinal Guidiccioni, who had previously expressed the view that there were enough Orders already and that they tended, after initial good intentions, to degenerate. But such was the force of the new proposals that even he accepted them. With Contarini's support, they submitted their rule to the Pope, Paul III, who commented, "The finger of God is here."

The aims of the Society, what today we would call a "mission statement", were clear and simple: "We have chosen to be called the Companions of Jesus and to fight under the flag of the Cross in the service of God in the Church. As to taking vows of poverty, chastity and obedience, we vow to go wherever the Pope may send us, in Europe or overseas, to defend and spread the True Faith. We will do this by preaching, teaching (instructing children in their religion), the Spiritual Exercises, saying Mass and going to the sacraments. We also want to work for those who are in need of help. All our tasks we will carry out free of charge."

The Bull concerning the new Society, *Regimini Militantis Ecclesiae,* was published on 27 September 1540. It was issued in the Palazzo San Marco by Cardinal Guidiccioni. The number allowed to join the new Society was initially fixed at sixty, but this limit was soon removed. However, the worldwide work of the Society had already begun. On 15 March 1540, at the request of the King of Portugal, Francis Xavier and Simón Rodriguez had left Rome for Portugal. Francis was to go to the new Portuguese colonies in India in April the following year and to undertake a missionary adventure that stunned the world.

The new Society had now to elect its Superior General: there could be only one choice. Francis Xavier had already left for India. Favre was in Germany, Rodriguez in Portugal, and Bobadilla in Calabria, but they had each already cast their votes. After their departure, Ignatius summoned his remaining companions, Laynez, Salmeron, Broët, Le Jay and Codure, to Rome for the election in Lent 1541. The vote was unanimous; Ignatius was elected Superior General of the new Society. He was fifty years old. In voting for him, Xavier wrote, "It is he who has fathered us together, at great cost of labour, and he will also know how to keep us, not without his cost, and to govern us to make us progress in virtue, for he knows each one of us better than any other."

Lainez wrote in more flowery terms, "Master Ignatius of Loyola, who having, according to the wisdom given him from God, begotten us all in Christ and fed us with milk while we were little, will, now that we are grown greater in Jesus Christ, direct and guide us with a substantial food of obedience into the pastures of paradise and the well of eternal life."

All, except Ignatius, voted for Ignatius, who wrote, "Myself excluded, I let the superior be the man who shall have the majority of votes." Alarmed by his election, he refused, was elected again, and returned to the monastery of San Pietro in Montorio, there to be advised by his confessor to accept, which he duly did.

On 22 April 1541, in an historic moment, the six companions walked to the Basilica of St Paul Outside-the-Walls. Full of emotion, they embraced each other and gave each other the kiss of peace. The Society was established, and their youthful promises and hopes at Montmartre in Paris had been fulfilled. The pilgrim years were over. For the next sixteen years, until his death, Ignatius was a prisoner at his desk and a constant administrator and letter-writer. From now until the end of his life, he would have to maintain an ever-growing correspondence with the increasing and widely scattered members of his Society. He was to write over seven thousand letters.

The first job Ignatius gave himself was to serve in the kitchen. In 1544 he moved to the house in Rome, which he had had built next to the Church of Santa Maria della Strada. Here, he would spend the rest of his life. One can still visit the small rooms where Ignatius lived, slept and received visitors. There was a balcony where he could look at the stars, free of Rome's present-day light pollution, and a small garden where he could walk.

Laynez was also working in Italy; a more prosaic task than going to the Indies, but just as important. He was later sent to work at the Council of Trent and became the second Father-General of the Jesuits, after Ignatius. Salmeron and Broët went to Ireland, where their lives were in danger and they were hunted men all the time. As Catholics, and particularly as Jesuits, their lives, or at least their freedom, were forfeit in a country that was officially Protestant despite its Catholic majority.

Francis Xavier was starting his great work in Goa. The heroic life of St Francis Xavier has been written about many times. He left Portugal for India in 1541, a voyage into the unknown which took thirteen months. The courage of the Portuguese navigators launching themselves, literally as they saw it, to the edge of the world, was staggering. Until 1544 Xavier concentrated on missionary work in India, and his Christian communities still survive him. From 1545 to 1547 he embarked upon a mission to the Moluccas in Indonesia and, in 1549 he arrived in Japan, starting an extraordinary adventure, only brought to its conclusion by massive persecution. He died in 1552, at the age of forty-six and utterly worn out, on a small island off the coast of China. Only five letters in ten years managed to reach him from Jesuit headquarters. What a man! What an amazing life of service! How sad that the last letter to him, summoning him home, never reached him. He was already dead, otherwise he might have met Ignatius one more time.

In Spain, Salmeron and Broët were opposed by the Dominican theologian Melchior Cano. He saw the Jesuits as yet another lax Order but, in time, such doubts were laid to rest, helped especially by the future Saint Francis Borgia.

Le Jay and Bobadilla were working for the Catholic princes in Germany. In 1550, Broët founded a new college at Clermont. Le Jay was sent to the Council of Trent and had to fight off attempts to make him a bishop. Peter Favre worked himself to death, after a few years travelling constantly between Germany, Spain and Portugal, giving The Spiritual Exercises, preaching and trying to convert the Protestant north of Germany. It was he who encouraged the two new recruits, Francis Borgia, a friend of Charles V, who gave up being Duke of Gandia and Viceroy of Catalonia, to be a humble Jesuit priest and became the third Father-General of the Jesuits, and Peter Canisius, who worked for the Counter-Reformation in Germany. He was one of the Jesuits who accepted that the Church needed reform and were influential in the Council of Trent (1545-1563), which marked a new beginning.

Simón Rodriguez, a friend of the King of Portugal, made good progress in Portugal. By Ignatius' death, 243 Portuguese men had started a lifetime's work which was to take them to the new colonies in India, Brazil and Africa.

Ignatius, though, took pains to keep his lifestyle modest. Rising early, saying Mass and going into the Church to teach the catechism, in very bad Italian, to children. Such was the force of his faith and the power of his teaching, people kept coming to hear him at Mass and go to him for Confession. During all this time, his major work was drawing up the Constitutions of his new Society. What he wanted to do was to create an organisation in which people submitted everything to pursuing the glory of God, and were not weighed down by other obligations.

Various religious orders are founded to carry out a particular duty. This was not Ignatius' aim. A Jesuit does not fulfil his life's work by caring for the sick, or singing the Divine Office, or just keeping silent and praying. All these things may help the Jesuit to reach his objective, but his objective is not any of these in themselves. The objective is the service of Jesus. A Jesuit, of course, has to surrender all his possessions and accept no honour or academic title, although many are very academically distinguished. They live in complete obedience to the Society, and their primary loyalty is not to each other per se, but to God.

In the early days of the Society there was no strict rule or way of life, or defined way of training novices. They simply took the month-long Exercises and worked in hospitals or at giving instruction with the catechism. Aided by his Secretary, Juan de Polanco, Ignatius sat in a small room dictating letters all day and using them as newsletters to maintain contact between the fast-growing and widely dispersed members of the Society.

He had to resist several efforts to make his Jesuits bishops. Broët was moved to say that he was called 'to poverty and not to honours'. Writing to King Ferdinand, Ignatius said, "The true and primitive spirit of this company is, in all simplicity, to go from city to city and from country to country for the greater glory of God and the salvation of souls, and not to confine its actions to any one particular province." Francis Borgia, for instance, had to turn down the offer of a Cardinal's Hat.

By the same token, attempts were made to stop his priests being appointed to the Inquisition in Portugal. Under pressure from the royal authorities, Ignatius relented and allowed his men to undertake this work, something which we may find distasteful now, but which was altogether more mainstream then.

Ignatius was no longer a shabby pilgrim, or would-be hermit, he was, *par excellence,* an administrator. This is the key to his success. He had always been more the careful child of Basque temperament, than the vague dreamer. This is why he succeeded in creating an efficient worldwide movement.

He still gave spiritual advice, but he would not ignore practical organisation – the opposite of St Francis of Assisi. Yet, he was still a misfit and could experience the same ecstasies and visions he had received at Manresa. After saying Mass he was so overcome with tears at the thought of the Trinity, and so profuse were his tears on occasions, that he feared he might go blind. His eyes would spontaneously fill with tears. He even had a vision, while saying Mass, of God the Father Himself, appearing to him like the sun. He was easily moved to rapturous contemplation of divine mystery. Sometimes, after Mass, he would sit enraptured for two hours, his face alight.

Meanwhile, he toiled away at the Constitutions of his new Society, trying to decide whether authority would flow mainly from the General of the Order, through national Superiors to the ordinary Jesuit priests, or whether the latter would have much more independence.

One practice that Ignatius encouraged in all the laity was regular Communion once a week, even daily, rather than once or twice a year, which had been the practice. Meanwhile, his companions were leaving him for duties abroad and gradually scattering around the world.

In 1549, Paul III, Ignatius' Protector, died at the age of eighty-three. Ignatius' own health, still affected by the mortifications at Manresa, was beginning to break down. Paul was succeeded by Julius III, who approved the new Constitution of the Order in 1550. When Julius

III died in 1555, he was succeeded for twenty-one days by Ignatius' friend, Pope Marcellus II.

Ignatius asked his companions if he could resign. They refused to let him go; he was too valuable. He was still to write over 6,000 letters in the last six years of his life. He also had the energy to fund a new international college, where students could be maintained before joining the Society. The idea was to have a four-year course in humanities, followed by a seven-year course in philosophy. Despite the fact that the members of the Society would be so well trained, he continued to insist that none should become bishops, which, he said, would be the ruin of the Society.

It would be wrong to suppose that Ignatius' principal intention was to counteract Lutheranism. The name Jesuit has become identified with the Counter-Reformation, but this would be too negative an interpretation of his work. There was, however, a lack of discipline in the fast-growing movement, and if nothing had been done, the new Society in Portugal might have been closed down by the authorities. Ignatius was prepared to deal harshly with people who disobeyed his instructions. In May 1555, a test of his leadership came when Cardinal Carafa, with whom he had clashed in Venice, was elected Pope. Ignatius physically trembled with dread in his rooms at the possibility of Carafa taking over, but the new Pope was to be fair to the Society. In any event, Ignatius' death was only a year off.

Rome

As his death approaches in this narrative, it is perhaps worthwhile to review the all-important years in Rome. When they arrived in Rome in November 1537, the companions had thought that their stay was going to be a temporary one. In fact, the prophecy of La Storta, "I will be favourable to you in Rome", was to come true. Not only was the Society founded there but, as also prophesied, Ignatius' life of pilgrimage was to end there. He was to spend longer there than anywhere else (nineteen years) till his death in 1556. In response to that prophesy, Ignatius had told one of his companions: "I do not know whether we shall be crucified in Rome". His crucifixion was to take the shape of being nailed to his desk for nineteen years, and to the ever greater burden of administering his new Society.

Their first home was lent to them by a certain Quirino Garzoni at Pinzio, near the Church of Trinita dei Monti. But, in June 1538, Ignatius, along with Pierre Favre, Diego Laynez and their other companions, moved into a new house near the Ponte Sisto.

His companions gave lectures, and Ignatius himself gave the Spiritual Exercises to a number of people, including Cardinal Farnese, Pope Paul III (1534-1549), who was a crucial influence in the early years of the new Society. Almost immediately, in November 1538, Ignatius had to defend himself directly in front of the Pope against accusations of heresy from the Augustine hermit Agostino Mainardi. In the same month, however, Pope Paul III gave the Society his verbal seal of approval. That same autumn the companions moved house again, to a property given them by the noble Frangipani family, near the Torre dei Merangolo.

November 1538 was a decisive moment. Ignatius realised, at the prompting of the Pope, that their future lay at home in Europe, "Why are you so anxious to go to Jerusalem? Italy is a good and true Jerusalem for you to work fruitfully in the Church of God".

On arriving in Rome, Ignatius had said to the people, "I see your windows are shut". In other words, the windows of their hearts were shut to suffering. He began, metaphorically, to throw them all open with his work among the poor and starving. It was an exceptionally cold winter in Rome that year. Hundreds were housed in the Jesuits' own home. People began to realise there was something new about this Society, that it was special and based on love, and they began to call the companions the "Pilgrims" or "Reformed Priests". There had, as yet, been no proper reform of Church or society in Europe. Requests began to come in for the Jesuits to work elsewhere in Europe, and even in the Indies. Being bound only by an oath of loyalty to the Pope, they were now to be scattered and their little brotherhood broken up.

Ignatius had said his first Mass on Christmas Day, 1538, in Santa Maria Maggiore. The decisive moment was approaching. In March 1539 Rodriguez had already been sent by the Pope to Portugal. The companions had debated their future and, in April 1539, were determined on creating a Society based on obedience to one of their number. Their group would be called the *Compania de Jesus,* or Company of Jesus. "Company" was used in its military sense. In those days a company was generally known by its captain's name, so that Ignatius and his followers were, by implication, soldiers of their captain, Christ. In the Latin Bull of their foundation, however, they were called *Societas Jesu.*

In April 1539, the Friends took Communion together to mark the firm decision they had made. Their ideas were put together by Ignatius in June in his *Summa Instituti,* which made clear that they would wear no special dress, nor sing in choir, meaning that unlike monks they would not sing the Divine Office at length every day. Although the Pope soon gave his initial approval, it took almost a year of lobbying in the curia before the Order was to be established firmly.

Then, in 1541, the new Society took over the control of the church of Santa Maria degli Astalli, and Ignatius was installed in the church as Superior General of the new Order. A home was built next door, where Ignatius lived for the rest of his life. For the next ten years, he laboured on the Constitutions (or rules) of his Society. The ban on increasing membership was lifted by Paul III in March 1544, and lay people and priests who were not fully professed members of the Society admitted in 1548. Ignatius was aided by a skilful secretary, Juan de Polanco. A new constitution was solemnly conferred by Pope Julian III in the Bull *Exposcit Debitum* in 1550.

In 1548, The Spiritual Exercises, written so many years before at Manresa, but continually improved and refined, were finally published. Though difficult to read, the Exercises were to transform the world. The book was the dynamo and the impetus of love and service of the Society's great spiritual leader. The Constitutions of the Society were the model drawn up by an assiduous and careful Basque nobleman to ensure there was a framework to the enthusiasm evoked by the Exercises.

In 1556, Ignatius was ill. In his judgement, and in the view of others, this was his death sickness. The thought of death brought him so much joy, and the comfort of death was now so overwhelming that he dissolved into tears. By the time of Ignatius' death, the Jesuits had founded forty-seven colleges in Europe. There was obviously no question of founding a college in England once Elizabeth had succeeded to the throne but, in 1593, Robert Persons, the colleague of the martyred

Jesuit Edmund Campion, founded a college for English Catholic students at St Omer. Some two hundred years later, during the French Revolution, the college was to move to its final home at Stonyhurst, Lancashire.

In 1551, a college was founded at Rome, soon moving to a building near San Stefano del Cacco. Ignatius was especially insistent that it should be free and Ignatian. The Roman College struggled, until Pope Gregory XIII guaranteed the fees of 200 students in 1584. Henceforth it was known as the Gregorian University, and still flourishes. Ignatius also founded a German college. In each of these great colleges, the rigorous, academic basis of the new reformed Church of the Counter-Reformation was to take shape.

Despite his ill health, these were wonderful years for Ignatius. His soul was very close to God. Philip Neri thought that a light sometimes flitted across his face. He described him as "The little Spaniard with a limp and shining eyes." He was reserved, yet greatly loved. But the Society still had to be administered, and by the time he died there were twenty houses alone in Italy, and nineteen elsewhere. He also spent many hours a day at prayer. He kept a copy of the New Testament and *Imitation of Christ* on his desk. He liked to look on all things at any time of the day as reminding him of God. Religion was not for one set time of the day, for Mass or a set of formal prayers. It was for all the day.

By July 1556 he was near death from liver disease. He asked his secretary Polanco to go to the Pope (Paul IV) for a last blessing. Polanco, not thinking the end was at hand, reminded him of the correspondence still to do. Typically, without complaining, Ignatius replied, "Do what you think best, I leave myself entirely in your hands." Later that night, a Brother heard him praying "Ay Dios!" – "Oh my God!" When they arrived at dawn the next day, July 31 1556, he was dying. Polanco hurried off through the empty streets of the Vatican for the blessing that Ignatius had asked for the day before. When he returned, Ignatius was already dead. There was no fanfare, and nothing special; he simply went quietly to the place where he wanted to be. His tomb was marked by a simple inscription: 'IGNATIUS LOYOLA FOUNDER AND FIRST FATHER-GENERAL OF THE SOCIETY OF JESUS. THIS STONE WAS PLACED BY HIS COMPANIONS AND SONS.'

At the time of his death, it was immediately and widely appreciated that a saint had died, although official recognition of such would have to wait. Even an old critic like Paul IV was moved. By 1587, Ignatius' grave had been moved to the Gesu in Rome, the site of a new church built by his Order. By 1609 he was beatified, and on March 12, 1622, with his friend, Francis Xavier, he was finally declared a saint. His own province of Guipuzcoa, asked that he become their patron saint.

In 1689 a new Baroque basilica was built around his home in Loyola and, in 1695, a great Baroque altarpiece was placed above his tomb in the Gesu. The Society lives on, four centuries after his death, under his motto, *Ad maiorem Dei gloriam:* "For the greater glory of God."

Ignatius was a small man, only five foot three. He limped and was often in poor health, but in these years the Society grew to a membership of 1,000, scattered over ten provinces. What was the secret of St Ignatius' success? It seems to be founded on his early training as a nobleman and courtier. He turned knightly virtues such as hard work, loyalty and courage to the service of God. But it couldn't be any old service, just doing the right thing – it had to be for the greater glory of God. It was this zeal, coupled with his friendliness, charm and willingness to help anybody, whatever their rank, which made him the natural leader of the Jesuits from the start. He was always the only choice, long before he was elected to any formal office. Above all he was patient, and he was willing to persevere in the task he set himself.

However, it would be quite wrong to think that after his conversion Ignatius was motivated in his religious vocation primarily by knightly virtues. He soon realised that the greatest attribute of a nobleman and knight – personal pride – must be conquered. In becoming effectively a wandering beggar and impoverished mature student, he was consciously surrendering his position and becoming nothing. He was deliberately imitating Christ in his humility. His Order's *raison d'être* was service to others, not itself, at the command not of its own Superior-General, but someone outside the order – the Pope. Everything now was not for him but for the greater glory of God – "A.M.D.G." *(Ad maiorem Dei gloriam)*.

By chance, I wrote the preceding words about the death of St Ignatius on 31 July, his feast day and the anniversary of his death.

Meditation: Society and work

I see your windows are shut. St Ignatius.
The body does not consist of one member but of many.
1 Corinthians 12:14.
They are of the world, therefore what they say is of the world,
and the world listens to them. 1 John: 4:5.

The best political thought is worthless compared to the most unanswered spiritual thoughts. There is no song without an echo; no joy needs to descend. The mere effort to put oneself mentally in God's presence is enough to produce happiness.

I meditated on this on a walk near my home. The country was nice but ordinary. I had some difficult people to deal with in a surgery. I thought how nice it would be if one could change one's job occasionally.

I must snap out of this and move on. I started by saying the Jesus prayer and the Rosary. The Sunday before, I had said the Joyful Mysteries as I walked in a glorious sunset along the fast-flowing River Hodder, in truly Tolkien territory. Indeed, that Lancashire countryside was said to have inspired Hobbiton.

Now, in my countryside, my mood brightened. I climbed a hill in the twilight. I sat down by some sheep. The scene was biblical in its simplicity. I imagined myself as their shepherd, not moving from these hills for weeks at a time. Time-slowing.

This was my country and I must appreciate it. This is my job and, like all jobs, it can become a chore, or one must view it as a prayer. Saint Giuseppe Moscati, a distinguished scientist and doctor, viewed every patient as a new prayer, almost a meditation. I cannot do that. I can pray in a church. When I arrive, little happens but, with time, a spiritual awakening dawns on me.

I can consciously create a prayer and a feeling of joy on a country walk. I cannot do it in a difficult meeting or surgery or crowded tube. But then I am not a saint.

We can only try.

Chapter 14
My Family and St Ignatius

My task of following in the footsteps of St Ignatius was almost done. It only remained for me to take my family to Rome, to see the place where he spent his last days, and to go there in the Jubilee Year 2000, to make a pilgrimage around the four great basilicas of St Peter St Mary Major, St John Lateran and St Paul Outside-the-Walls and of course, St Ignatius and the Gesu. Then the task would be complete.

On this last stage of our pilgrimage, we travelled by car to Rome, two thousand miles, with six children in the back. We left on a cloudy Wednesday in August and stayed the night in a youth hostel in Boulogne. The next day we drove south to Combloux in the French Alps. The motorway doglegs around the Montagne de Rheims and we came off it to drive through the Champagne vineyards, in sun and heat. Every day for the next three weeks was to be one of brilliant sunshine. On every side spread rows of vineyards and tiny narrow tractors on high wheels threaded their way through unseen paths across the hills.

At the Rheims service station, the car had decided to start leaking liquid over the forecourt of the supermarket. I drove around to the Toyota garage and, with my comic-like technical approach, had to try to explain what was wrong. I nearly poured the suspension oil into the engine. Luckily, I was stopped in time by an incredulous Frenchman.

We arrived at Mary's sister's chalet in the French Alps and went to bed. From the bedroom we had a view of the great array of peaks stretching away from us. On the Saturday morning we drove through the Fréjus tunnel and on to the flat northern Italian plain, to arrive at our home for the next two weeks. The journey of Ignatius' companions to Northern Italy had taken several weeks. Along the way they argued with travelling companions and with Calvinists. Our journey had taken a few hours and we argued together about more mundane things.

We had come to stay in the northern Tuscan hills, before going on to Rome and the final part of the quest for St Ignatius. I was feeling unaccountably depressed. Perhaps it was because, on July 20th, I had turned fifty. Perhaps it was the thought, as lots of people feel at that same age, that my career was not going anywhere very fast. Suddenly, two things of interest happened.

Tamara, my daughter, had been sick in the middle of the night. I could not sleep, so I got up to open the window and looked at a brilliant starlit sky across the valley, to the great mountains of the French Alps and the range around Mont Blanc. Such views expand the mind. As I gazed at it, I recalled Anthony Beevor's book *The Spanish Civil War* which I had finished reading whilst on the train coming back from St Beuno's. It depressed me, but I found it fascinating. When I got home I immediately picked up Hugh Thomas's *The Spanish Civil War*, which had been lying around unread for many years.

At St Beuno's I had also read more on St Ignatius. Along with St Teresa of Avila, he was one of the contributors towards the greatness of Spain, which, for a time in the sixteenth century and onwards, joined the select club of nations that could be described as the greatest on earth. The Spanish Civil War, it seemed, was an elemental struggle between the Spain of St Ignatius and the Jesuits supporting the Catholic religion on the one hand, and the Spain of Liberalism – democracy, the Communist Party, and the largest Anarchist trade union then in existence in Europe, on the other.

The Jesuits were expelled by the Republic (the left-wing Spanish government of the 30s), and up to seven thousand priests were murdered during the Spanish Civil War (1936-39) because they happened to find themselves on the wrong side of the lines. There were horrible massacres and executions – indeed, on both sides – and it could be argued on these grounds that neither side was better than the other. I had assumed that my sympathies were with the Nationalist side, because the Republicans were associated with atheistic Communism. But increasingly, as I read Beevor's book, my views became more equivocal.

Like Anthony Eden, the British Foreign Secretary of the time, I began to believe that the views most closely approximated to my own were those of the Basques during the Civil War. The Basques were, of course, brutally put down by the Nationalists, and the bombing of Guernica has become a symbol of the Civil War. But, the Basques were the only Republicans who kept their churches open and did not imprison or kill the local priests. What most struck me about the War was the depth of animosity, indeed sheer hatred, between the classes and factions.

In Europe it seems to us that we have increasingly solved the problem with the creation of the welfare state. That is a compromise between the aspirations of the working class and the bourgeoisie. The first is given adequate state health, education and employment prospects, as well as a social security network that prevents the worst effects of the kind of poverty that we knew in the past. The latter, the bourgeoisie, are allowed to get on with increasing their own personal wealth, acquiring property and running their businesses and professions much as they want to.

It seems to me that such a compromise, which is basically Social, or Christian, Democracy, makes sense. If it works for us in the developed world, why cannot it make sense in our relationship with the Third World? Perhaps we are making the same mistake with poverty in the Third World, which the bourgeoisie made with poverty on their own doorstep in the first part of the last century.

So that night at Combloux, as I looked out across the valley to the mountains, I felt sure that I should go back to England and argue for a far greater effort to help the Third World. Not just out of self-interest for the developed world, or even because it is the right thing to do, but because the consequences of not doing anything could be disastrous. There could well be the same kind of explosions that led to millions of dead under the Russian Revolution and Fascist dictatorships of the first fifty years of the last century.

It seems to me though, that rather than adopt a tax-and-spend approach, we should try and involve the public, perhaps by giving tax relief up to a higher level than is already allowed for charitable donations, especially for giving to Third World countries. This would cost the state money, but it would be right, both for moral reasons and those of self-interest.

I also felt that one shouldn't just talk about these things once a month or so, when subjects of international development were coming up in discussion, but to do so more often. Third World issues and the huge amount of poverty throughout much of the world impinge on many other areas where we are over-generous to ourselves, for instance, in terms of how much we spend on health and education in our own prosperous countries.

Therefore my interests in Spain, and in St Ignatius as the creator of one part of modern Spain, had come full circle, to an interest in the social and political concerns of my own times, and issues of moderation and tolerance. Not themes, perhaps, that would have immediately recommended themselves to Ignatius. They reminded me of the words of the twentieth century Spanish philosopher, Unamuno, who summed it up best – whilst supporting the Nationalists in the Civil War he decided to speak out against their excesses, in favour of the virtues of a more moderate approach.

An Anarchist leader, again during the Civil War, spoke of his belief in the fraternity of Jesus Christ, rather than the tyranny of the Church. Now the Jesuits, at the end of the twentieth century, had themselves moved from a rigid defence of Catholic orthodoxy to speaking out above all for the poor of the world, and perhaps they had a point. They are no longer associated with an inquisitorial approach, but more that of a social conscience.

At the thought of what one could do, my depression started to lift. This thinking made me also consider something that I had often thought about in the past

– the need for some kind of movement for what I call 'an open monastery'. It is an incredibly valuable part of Eastern spiritual practice that people can enter and leave a Buddhist monastery for a time as a monk, without a lifelong commitment, and thereby recharge their spiritual batteries.

In the West, many monasteries and convents – with the exception of the more traditional ones – are dying. Not many young people want to devote themselves to a life, staying in the one place, based on poverty and celibacy. However, in the hustle and bustle of consumerism and materialism of the modern world, more and more people do want to *visit* monasteries, and they want to feel more a part of what is going on, and not just go for a weekend or on retreat for a week. They want to do more than just attend the services, eat in the refectory and then leave; they want to feel more a part of the monastic community.

True, one can become an Oblate, a kind of supporter of the monastery whilst living in the real world. But I think it would be a breakthrough if the monasteries could encourage people to take one step further, so that they could join the community without a commitment and to stay there for whatever length of time they so wished. Whilst there, they would be, in terms of lifestyle, full members of the community. They would be required by the Abbot or Superior to work in the garden, or do any other jobs, attend the services, and eat with the other monks or nuns. They would also be allowed to spend some time in the monks' enclosure, chatting with the permanent members of the community. Gradually, they could thus become a real part of the community, but still without any long-term commitment. Perhaps they would come back every year, for a weekend or a week.

I have often wondered how such a movement could be created, and whether other people are thinking of it. While I was sitting at St Beuno's trying to write up my notes on St Ignatius, I was determined to approach at least one person in the monastic community, whom I knew well, with the idea. This was another inspiration that came from this pilgrimage of St Ignatius, but it's an idea that has yet to be realised.

After about a week of staying in Italy, I began to feel frustrated that, in the great heat, I seemed to spend most of my time in swimming pools. It is perhaps the "sensible" thing to do, but I started to read – or to try and read – the New Testament from beginning to end, starting with the Gospel of St Matthew. After all, this was supposed to be a pilgrimage and I found it soothing.

One day, in Lucca, I saw a very old man, bent almost double, walking. He reminded me of someone. He looked rather like Mgr Alfred Gilbey – an elderly priest I knew – in his later years, just before he died. The important thing about this man in Lucca was that, despite his very great age, he was keenly interested in everything going on about him. He was stopping and looking in every shop window. As he raised his head from his stooped back, I saw this as a sign that we should never give up, however old and ill we are. We should never stop taking an interest in things about us. Even if we are closer to ninety than eighty, as this old man seemed to be, and even if we are simply passing a shop window full of clothes for young people, as he was. This old gentleman refused to give up.

While the others went to the supermarket just outside the ramparts at Lucca, I walked around on my own, ending up at the Church of San Fernando in the northern part of the old city. I sat in the chapel of St Zita. I knelt before her remains and said that I would try not to be critical of other people in the future, a promise that, of course, I promptly broke with my family. But the thought occurred very strongly to me. Why at that moment in the chapel of St Zita, I do not know.

The days in our hilltop village passed very quickly. We had no garden, or only a very small one, and that was overgrown and hemmed in by other buildings. Some mornings I walked out along the path to the end of the village, beyond the Via de Castello, and sat in the shade of a small hut. I looked out over the valley beyond Bagha de Lucca, to the distant hills and mountains of the Italian Alpini, either reading a novel, or trying to read the Gospel of St Matthew.

We spent five days on and off by the seaside. Much as I loved the sea, by the end of those five days I got fed up with the orderliness of the beach at Viareggio, yet another Italian resort, and the self-regard of the Italians for their fine clothes and their good looks, crowds of them improving their suntans on the beach. I looked forward to something quieter and shadier.

We spent one day walking in Florence, in suffocating heat and humidity. It must have been something like 40 degrees Celsius. I queued up for over an hour to get into the Uffizi Gallery, but it was well worth it, walking through the cool rooms, not too overcrowded, looking at never-ending pictures of the Virgin and Child which had been painted through the centuries. Even the children seemed to show some interest.

On my last visit to Lucca, I walked to the Cathedral. The streets were wide and cool and empty, and indeed, after Florence, it was easy to find one's way around, due to their distinctive differences one from another. There was also plenty of shade. I walked through a huge billowing curtain into the cool of the Cathedral and sat alone for a few minutes, while the others stayed in the car.

One evening, after a day at the seaside, we went to the Piazza dei Miracoli in Pisa, just as the sun was going down. Of course it was invaded by tourists, but the light was so beautiful that they seemed to vanish beside the Cathedral baptistery and the famous leaning tower.

On another day we escaped from the beaches along the flat Tuscan coast and went to the beach of Lerici, on the Italian Riviera, where the mountains fall right down into the sea. There we sat on a small strip of sand. Here there was no private beach, everyone was positioned higgledy-piggledy. The children dived off rocks, and everything seemed more natural and, somehow, more spiritual than the other more ordered beaches.

Meditation: Family

This is the message which you have heard from the beginning, that we should love one another. 1 John: 3:11.

At Mass today the reading was from St Matthew's gospel: "Go and be reconciled with your brother first and then come back and present your offering." The priest asked us if we were often irritable, if we had difficulty in mucking in and going along with the stream. If we do, is there something wrong at the heart of our spiritual life?

How can I live at all times with the injunction, "This is the message that you heard from the beginning, that you should love one another"? Waking back in the sunshine, some irritable thought crossed my mind. Why am I always so impotent in my work?

"Accept" came back the word. Accept where you are now, what you are. Accept that there will be others younger and greater than you, as there will be others older and lesser than you, as they must accept you.

If we can do this, we may rub along in our families, in our communities, in our nations.

Try "accepting" yourself. It can do wonders.

I believe; help my unbelief! Mark 9:24.

Three nights in a row I had had wonderful dreams. I had no dream tonight, but I felt my chest hurting slightly. What if I were to die now? I saw a white light. I did not yet walk towards it, but I would have been happy to do so.

I had done enough.

You might try using dreams. Many people say to me that they never remember their dreams, but, with a bit of effort it is possible. If you pray before you go to sleep, make a conscious effort to remember with a memory jog something when you wake. Something might happen. Give it a go.

Chapter 15
Rome 2000 – Jubilee Year

It was now time to start the last part of our family pilgrimage. We had spent a hot, tiring morning packing up the small house at Lucca, leaving at around 2pm. By the time we were on the *autostrada* (motorway), the temperature gauge told me that it was climbing to 39 degrees Celsius. Everybody was tired and hot. The windows were wide open, but all they let in was a blast of hot air, as if one was standing inside a fan-powered oven. We stopped at a town in order to look for a swimming pool. In spite of the signs pointing to a *Piscina*, we failed to find it.

Should we stop en route at Orvieto? I rang up a hotel, the Albergo de Duomo. No answer. Not surprising, since when we arrived it was being refurbished and every window was out. We pressed on to Rome, arriving in the sticky night at a depressing – or what seemed to be a depressing – pensione. It was on the sixth floor of a large office block, around a courtyard, with a rickety old Victorian lift in which one had to open two doors and stand in a cage.

We spent the night sweating in a room overlooking a yard. The next day there was a discussion about the price of the hotel. Even two rooms would cost us £700 for four days. Mary was quite rightly agitated. I decided to ring the youth hostel, but they were not keen on children, and anyway, only had communal dormitories – I felt a bit too old to be sleeping in a communal dormitory with eighteen-year-olds, so we stayed in our *pensione*.

On Sunday morning we walked to St Peter's, which was only half a mile away. We could see its Dome from one of our bedroom windows. We pushed our way into the basilica which can hold six thousand, and there must have been all of that number there at 11 am that Sunday. Everybody was hot and bothered, even inside the basilica, which I had hoped would be cool. It was difficult to make any kind of sense out of the Mass that was going on, burbling in the distance, with thousands of people milling around. We emerged, and had lunch at a so-called 'self-service café'. Costing the best part of £100 for a family, we had a few dollops of rice on a plastic plate. Mary had a fit and we left. Not the best moment. What were we to do?

We decided to finish the pilgrimage there and then, by going to visit the three other basilicas. We drove first to Santa Maria Maggiore (St Mary Major) and spent the next three or four hours moving on to San Giovanni in Laterano (St John Lateran) and finally, San Paulo fuori le Mura (St Paul Outside-the-Walls). Every time, as the pilgrimage demanded, I walked in through the 'Santa Porta', the Holy Door.

The basilicas were cool and soothing, and because when I first arrived it was lunchtime, St Mary Major was almost completely empty. Even Theodore and Nicholas running up and down the nave didn't do too much to disturb the peace. I walked around the cloisters of St Mary Major and the other basilicas. They were empty, peaceful and carved in Roman marble. However, I was still looking for St Ignatius' church. So, I asked the priest at St Mary Major where Santa Maria della Strada (Our Lady of the Way) was, because I knew this was the church that St Ignatius had taken over when he first moved to Rome in 1537.

The priest did not know – why should he? There are many churches in Rome, and he didn't come from Rome. It would have been rather difficult for him to know its whereabouts in any case because, as I subsequently discovered, Santa Maria della Strada had been knocked down five centuries before, when, in 1564, after Ignatius' death, the Jesuits began to build the Gesu, which stands on the site of the older church. I still had no idea where Ignatius' house was, but I thought that if I made my way to the Gesu, I might find out. What the priest could do, however, was to hear my Confession. Having been absolved and done my penance, I asked for a good pilgrimage to help me overcome all the problems of taking six children on such a long car journey.

On the way back from St Paul Outside-the-Walls, I stopped at what I thought was the Gesu. It was a part of Rome where the great churches almost abut each other, with just a few streets in between them. In fact, the church that I was visiting was Santa Maria sopra Minerva, which had a wide nave and a restful blue ceiling.

In the evening, we went to McDonald's, where the children ate hamburgers, and Marina's scooter was promptly stolen. It was quite a change of scene. After finding the false Gesu earlier, I had walked around the block and found the church of 'Sant'Ignazio'. I walked in and saw the magnificent fresco on the ceiling, with the light radiating through the image of Ignatius and his followers. Some would find it a bit over the top, but it is undeniably a masterpiece of Baroque art.

The next day we spent two-and-a-half hours wandering through the Forum, while I tried to explain the old ruins to my daughters, and they became increasingly irritated at my ineptitude. Afterwards, we took refuge in a swimming pool in the middle of the 'EUR' (Esposizione Universale Roma), a complex of 1930s buildings, which originally had been the creation of Mussolini to celebrate twenty years of fascism in Italy.

I took the train back early in a crowded metro and wandered around on my own, up and down various streets and into quiet churches. One of my favourites was *Santa Maria in Trivio* (Our Lady at the Crossing of Three Roads). Behind a substantial façade was yet another Baroque masterpiece, albeit a tiny one. It was empty, but there was music playing, and somebody had left out three copies of the Gospel of Luke for the Jubilee. I started to read one of them, along with the Psalms, and the book of Amos. I wandered back through the streets to the Church of Sant'Ignazio, where the family were waiting. There we had one of our most successful *al fresco* meals of the holiday. Later, I walked them all back through to the Trevi fountain and showed them *Santa Maria in Trivio*. By this time everybody was getting tired and just wanted to go home.

On the Tuesday, our last full day in Rome, I was, as usual during the tail-end of my holidays, tramping the streets looking for money from a bank as the cash machines were not working. I finally found a bank and withdrew some money. I arrived at the back of the Vatican Museum at 1 pm to find vast crowds. I shuffled through, exhausted. Mary, seemingly on the edge of a breakdown, was to be revived by the walls of the Sistine Chapel. It is extraordinary how this titanic work of Michelangelo, his Last Judgement and Creation, still has the power to inspire awe after all these centuries. I am not sure what the children thought of it, but perhaps even they felt a tiny bit chastened.

After another fruitless search for a swimming pool, I persuaded the others, tired and hot, to let me drive to the home of St Ignatius. I had found out the day before that it was indeed next to the Gesu. This was a haven of peace. There were very few people there. I was struck by the great simplicity of the man. His plain cloak and vest are exhibited, as is a copy of his death mask, set at his correct height. As mentioned before, he was a tiny man, only five foot three.

I walked through the low rooms thinking of this simple life of a man who had completely renounced worldly goods. The simplicity of the room was pleasant, after all the crowds and Baroque splendour of the rest of Rome. I finally came to the small room where Ignatius spent the last seventeen years of his life, writing, sleeping and receiving visitors in this one tiny space. It was a suitable end to the pilgrimage.

Seeing Ignatius' old room reminded me of the key to true happiness: the renunciation of what most people think the most important things in their life, namely property or material possessions of one type or another. This is what gives those few who achieve it true freedom. Most of the house where Ignatius lived was, of course, knocked down long ago, but his own rooms – a small chapel which he visited and in which he died, his bed-sitting room and a small room for a lay brother who looked after him in his last years – are still preserved. My memory has an impression of stone-tiled floors, white walls, and wooden beams.

When Ignatius arrived in Rome in 1537, he deliberately chose this spot at the centre of the city, which then had only about fifty thousand people living in it. In those days the Pope did not live all the time in the area of St Peter's, but quite often in the Palazzo Venezia, behind the site that Ignatius chose for his headquarters. A short walk from here could take him to the civic centres, the Papal Court, the prosperous areas, and, indeed, to the Jewish Ghetto and the numerous slums. This is where Ignatius first set out to work amongst the poor and to run his growing Society, writing and dictating thousands of letters. In contrast to the simplicity of the three rooms where Ignatius lived (about eight hundred square feet in all), the Jesuits, in around 1680, commissioned a member of their Order, Brother Andrea Pozzo, to decorate the corridor with extraordinarily ornate frescoes.

What struck me most of all about Ignatius' room was its utter plainness: just two small cabinets for storage, and his desk. This furniture is old and threadbare, eaten half away by rot or woodworm. It brings home forcefully again how unimportant material possessions are – it did for about half an hour or so anyway. I was alone at first, but then Natalia and Mary joined me, and we walked out slowly together.

The pilgrimage, then, was finally over. Afterwards, we sat on the steps of the fountain opposite the Pantheon (a beautiful and well-preserved building, once a Roman temple, but since the seventh century a church where Mass is still said to this day). We stayed and watched for a while as the crowds went by. Then, as we walked to the Spanish Steps and tried to buy a guide book to Rome, my Visa card was refused. We had come back to worldly "reality". After a long wander around we managed to find a parking space (something unheard of in Rome). We had supper outside in the Piazza Navona, a huge space packed with tourists and providing a complete contrast to where we had been hours before.

On our last day, the Wednesday, we got up early to walk to St Peter's Square for our audience with the Pope, along with about five thousand other people. We took our seats on the *Reparto Speciale,* reserved for us by the secretary of the British Ambassador to the Holy See. We thought there would be a long wait, but soon there was great excitement as the Pope was driven through the crowds in his Popemobile and up a ramp to his chair. A stooped man, weakened by illness, but still with a powerful message. It was baking hot. As I sat in the open sun, the sweat was pouring off me. Then he spoke, in six languages: English, German, Italian, Spanish, Portuguese, and Czech. Afterwards, we needed to go to a café, to cool off with some coffee and Sprite, and then back to our hotel, to finally pack the car and leave.

We drove up through Italy to Savona, on the coast near Genoa. The aim was to drop off briefly at Turin before tackling the Alps. As we were approaching the town, I started reading the guide book. I had already said to the children that Turin was the place where the Shroud of Jesus was kept, but that there was no chance of us seeing it because it was only opened or displayed every twenty years. When I opened the guide book it said that it was going to be displayed for the Jubilee from 12 August to 20 October. The last occasion it was displayed, there were crowds of people but, of course, since then it has been carbon-dated, and there is apparent evidence that suggests it dates from the thirteenth or fourteenth century (though the validity of this test has since been disputed by some scientists). We walked through huge tents obviously designed for vast throngs of people, virtually alone. It was still a moving moment to see this amazing icon. I was asked to say a few words on behalf of the official English pilgrimage, for which they gave me a text.

We emerged and had lunch in a café, and then drove slowly out of the city, out of Italy, and over the Alps, back to stay with Mary's aunt in Switzerland. This truly was the end of our pilgrimage and, for the time being at least, the end of the relationship of my family with St Ignatius. My journey in search of St Ignatius was over.

Meditation:
Rome – submitting to authority

After I have been there, I must also see Rome. Acts 19:21.

The word "Rome" conjures up notions of authority and obedience to the Pope. The Jesuits were founded in obedience to the Pope as his "shock troops". Are people nowadays – am I – happy with my conscience being determined by one man?

But authority is more comforting. Are we not happier in assuming the rightness of something, instead of endlessly questioning it?

At the end of the day, we can only pray. Sending out our prayers into the unknown. Trusting to God. We can only hope that eternity is listening. If we lose this hope, then hope itself is lost and there is only despair. The assumption of hope is the essence of joy.

See for yourself. Forget authority and "assume" belief or hope.

PART TWO

Chapter 1
The Spiritual Exercises

St Beuno's is a Jesuit Retreat House set in the Clwyd valley of North Wales. It is an old seminary, in a stark Gothic building with gardens rising behind it. One September afternoon after my trip to Spain, I travelled there by train. One can do the full thirty-day Spiritual Exercises, but, with all my family commitments, I had only one week.

What are the Spiritual Exercises? They are the notes that Ignatius jotted down in his exercise book during his time at Manresa, perhaps sitting in the cave above the River Cardoner. He viewed them literally as exercises. Indeed, in his Introduction he actually compares them with running or walking, but they are intended to try to promote a better understanding of one's spiritual state.

The problem is that if you just go to a bookshop and buy a translation, it is virtually unreadable, even though it is just a thin book. The language is antique to say the least. Ignatius' basic concept was that you should spend thirty days over them, a full four weeks. During the first week, he invites us to reflect on our sins, perhaps be moved to embarrassment or shame by them, and in the second week, having established our own weakness, we should follow the life of Christ and feel its attractiveness, so that we might find some strength to turn away from the way we live at present. During the third week, we should contemplate the Passion, crucifixion and death of Jesus. During the fourth week, we should contemplate His Resurrection and Ascension and how these restore mankind's relationship with God through the forgiveness of sins. Some people might take a full four weeks; some might take less, others more.

Ignatius didn't expect people to do these retreats on their own. He developed the concept of a daily individual meeting with a retreat director, in which one could be given readings for the day, and then live through them and make progress that way. This has formed the basis of Ignatian retreats ever since.

I clearly wasn't going to understand him at all unless I attempted some sort of retreat. Ignatius recognises that many people (perhaps most) are too busy to leave their homes and their work for a full thirty days, and therefore, in his famous nineteenth annotation, he provides for a retreat within ordinary life.

My Retreat Director during my week at St Beuno's was to be Sister Helen. We agreed the normal format of me going to see her every morning. The first item of the text that one prays over in such a retreat is the principle and foundation set down at the beginning of the first week of The Spiritual Exercises: "Man is created to praise, reverence, and serve God Our Lord, and by this means to save his soul. The other things on the face of the earth are created for man and that they may help him in prosecuting the end for which he is created. From this it follows that man is to use these things in as much as they help him on to his end, and ought to rid himself of them so far as they hinder him." This is a great claim.

My whole life and every day should be part of a worship of God.

"For this it is necessary to make myself indifferent to all created things in order that He is allowed the choice of my free will so that, on my part, I want not health rather than sickness, riches rather than poverty, honour, rather than dishonour, a long rather than a short life, and so in all the rest; desiring and choosing only what is most conducive for me to the end for which I am created."

The key to the exercise is to contemplate that last paragraph. Can we really be indifferent to all these things: good health, being well off, being well thought of, living a long time, and all the rest? The answer, of course, is that most of us can't. But it doesn't mean that we can't think about how this is the route to true fulfilment and happiness.

That night I noted down what had passed on the first day, and I realized that my whole life was filled with anxieties. Even on this little trip to the retreat, I was anxious that I had forgotten to bring an alarm clock, and worried if I would wake up in time. I was anxious that I had cut too large a slice of bread at breakfast and it had got stuck in the toaster, despite the notice on the side saying "Do not cut thick slices and put them in the toaster." I was anxious yesterday that I might miss the train here. And there were other anxieties. I was anxious that my son would not receive a place in his first choice of school, and so end up in an indifferent comprehensive.

There were fears too – fears that there may be some terrible cancer lurking unseen inside me. There were also doubts, doubts that God exists at all. At times I even wondered whether our souls are simply the products of a few chemical and electrical impulses that are extinguished on death.

I had jealousies, jealousies for those who were talked about and acclaimed in my work, where I am not. I also had wants: wanting a bigger house where we are not falling over each other all the time; and irritations: I was irritated that the builder in my home had just destroyed the only few fruit trees I have ever owned and dumped 400 tons of earth on the lawn. I was despising people because they are stupid or ordinary. I desired what I could not have. All these anxieties, fears, wants, desires, jealousies, irritations, doubts… St Ignatius tells us to be indifferent to them all.

How, I asked myself as I noted down my thoughts after the first day of the retreat (as a kind of examination of conscience), could I hold them in balance as an integral part of my life? To value them, dismiss them and enjoy them, as I enjoyed the success of passing a professional exam just this week. I asked myself if I had the faith and the strength to see them all as God's work.

Could I see his beauty everywhere? Could I see it in the sun passing over the Vale of Clwyd? Could I also see God's beauty in the hideous motorway cutting across it within half a mile of where I was standing, looking out across the Vale to the distant mountains of Snowdonia? As I sat there, I tried to imagine what St Ignatius had felt in the early days of his conversion. I realised it was what I was now trying to feel myself: that to save one's soul, the innermost core and animator of one's entire being, one must praise everything in the world as God's work and come to believe sincerely that it is beautiful. To glorify the world is to glorify God.

St Ignatius assures us that we cannot progress towards God unless we throw off the shackles of fear, want and dislike that hold us down. The question is: how do we do this? Surely, the only way is to put God first? Can one even complete one day without being vexed about someone else? The most difficult thing in life is to deny self. In the words at the beginning of Ignatius' Spiritual Exercises, can one really be prepared to endure sickness rather than health, poverty rather than riches, or even than comfort? Dishonour rather than honour, and a short rather than a long life?

At the moment, I had to tell myself that, in all honesty, I could not. True, I was only at the beginning, but the truth is that I will never be able to achieve the relationship with God that Ignatius achieved. But I did begin to see that, if I was to make progress, I had to believe that at the heart of everything is a God whose love for me is unconditional and whose love I must reciprocate.

The less burdened I was by anxiety and fear, the greater chance love would be a constant in my life. The only way to overcome fear would be to embrace God's love and accept it as personal to oneself.

I began to see that what Ignatius was telling me was that I would always want to have health, long life, honour and riches, but, by themselves, compared to the infinity of God, they were like grains of sand compared to the universe. I should take them and enjoy them if they came, but I should forget them if they went. If I held these things in their true perspective then they would not define the choices I made in life, they could be part of the really interesting and important goal of life, seeking God.

All I really had to do was to ask myself, "Does this thought, or action, or word, or deed, help me in my path towards God, or does it hinder me?" If it helped me, I should accept it and pursue it. If it hindered, I should reject it, and usually one knows the difference.

I found difficulty meditating all day in the different chapels of the retreat house. I was lying awake, and suddenly it came to me in the middle of the night – not only joy and peace, but also fulfilment coming from the presence of God, and a feeling that I would be looked after until death. This intense feeling was no dream. It was a real conscious understanding which I had to set down there and then, and which I did, at 2.53 am. Finally, the clock on the pager came into its own. I could check the time and know it was no dream. The insight came to me when I was just having a trivial thought about whether I would have to attend a business lunch after the retreat, and I started to ask myself why I was there.

Mere proofs of God, rational ideas about the creation of the universe, were not enough. One looked for a feeling of *joy* at the presence of God, and it came, and I owed it to a prosaic thought about whether or not I should invite somebody to a lunch. Profound thoughts can often come out of trivial ones.

As I completed my first day of an Ignatian retreat, I was happy. I felt I had made some progress, only small progress admittedly, because my experience was far less intense and concentrated and far more short-lived than that of Ignatius. But progress, nevertheless, into understanding the thought processes of St Ignatius five centuries before.

On the second day, I read out to Sister Helen what I had achieved during my first day of trying to hold things in balance. It was my modern interpretation of Ignatius' indifference to health and honour and riches.

She talked to me about the third day of the first week of The Spiritual Exercises, and of the five Exercises that Ignatius suggests: to think about the fall of the angels; of the expulsion from the Garden of Eden; of comparing my sinfulness to what Christ has done for me on the Cross.

Sister Helen gave me from day five a text of Luke's story of the Prodigal Son and a copy of Rembrandt's picture to compare my sinfulness to God's love. She wanted me to ponder on this. This is the technique of "visiting" a Gospel scene, which was a new concept in meditation introduced by Ignatius. She told me that the Exercises of St Ignatius might be more suitable to a young cleric of the sixteenth century – thinking about them in the morning, the afternoon or the evening, and even the middle of the night. But what I tried to achieve in these five days would be a taste of what they were about, and therefore, an insight into the mind of St Ignatius. The first week is about repentance, which means accepting God's invitation to come out of sin.

That afternoon in our discussions I talked about sin and the evil spirit within us that imprisons us, as contained in Section 313 of the Exercises. The example Ignatius uses is when a lover advises a woman he is seducing "Don't tell anyone" – just so we try and bottle things up; or when the evil spirit within us tries to gain entry through the part of our being which we thought was stronger. We talked about Ignatius' visit to Montserrat, of his being advised by the priest there to consider his sin, and being so tormented by guilt that eventually he felt like throwing himself into a pit and killing himself, but coming out of his despair by pondering on God's love. So I meditated on Luke and the story of the Prodigal Son and prayed the Colloquy, Ignatius' noble verses in the Exercises, asking to live a life in search of God.

This day, then, was about my sinfulness and the realisation that to overcome it is a lifelong process, but realising also that sin can be transformed into a new life.

I read chapter 6 of Jesuit priest Gerard Hughes' *God of Surprises,* which confronted me with this view. "I despise a person who thinks only of himself, his wealth and security. Should I not also despise the nation that gives the minimum to the poorest nations?" Is Ignatian spirituality primarily something personal or does it have a wider social application?

Was Ignatius preaching only to the individual soul saving itself and finding God? I think he was, but to the extent that if more and more people live a life more tolerant and loving of others, society will be saved.

Ignatius gained his first insights by reading Ludolph of Saxony, whose technique was very visual. He asks us to put ourselves at the foot of the cross, beside the manger and in front of the saints. I increasingly feel that I can only really understand Ignatius through a visual medium, through finding something that compares my life and my seeking with his.

I left Sister Helen and started to read Gerard Hughes. I felt put off at the start because he seemed to want to blame me for not being a unilateral nuclear disarmer, but I moved on and made progress. What I thought particularly useful was his concept of living the parable of the Prodigal Son and trying to act it out in one's mind. I walked for a little and started the process. I thought of my sins and shortcomings but soon came to a stop because I could not feel sufficiently sorry for them.

St Ignatius had thought of hurling himself into a pit at Montserrat because of what he felt was the enormity of his sin. Last week, I had felt depressed at the destruction of my garden, certainly not to the extent of hurling myself into a pit, and not because of my own sin, but because of one of life's many frustrations. After lunch, I read through Fleming's modern translation of St Ignatius for the first week and prepared myself for my walk. As I walked, I started to ponder on what Ignatius tells us to think about, namely the fallen angels, beings which still do rebel against God, not for any sin of the flesh, but of the spirit. I thought about the small sin of Adam and Eve that resulted in the fall of the world. They were offered paradise; they chose sin. There was only one rule they had to keep, and they broke it. I pondered hell and became ashamed. Hell is for people who say no. But I still did not feel sufficiently sorry, even saying the Colloquy before the Cross, imagining Jesus before me; but still, I had tried to seek him as Ignatius asked me to do.

I then continued to think about Luke's parable of the Prodigal Son, and of the moment when he sets out to return home. At that point some light dawned upon me. He went home to his father – not because he was sorry, he was not – but he sought his father to forgive him. Thus I felt I was slowly returning to God, and to Christ, his manifestation on earth, and that he would forgive me for myself, even though at this stage, I was imperfect in my sorrow for my sins, indeed was not really sorry at all.

I thought of some other readings that Sister Helen asked me to think about. For instance, Psalm 103. One's life is like grass, but as a father has compassion for his children, so the Lord has compassion for me. I ended up by pondering on Luke's Gospel, "Lord if you choose, you can make me clean." I do choose.

As I walked, turning over in my mind these parables and readings, I slowly climbed the mountain behind St

Bueno's retreat centre, Moel Maenefa. At the very top, in the midst of glorious views was a rotting sheep, its ribcage exposed. Nobody had bothered to clear it away. St Ignatius would have enjoyed the symbolism – in life we are close to death.

As I descended towards the valley, the sun lowering in the West, glorious views of bracken, fir-trees and rolling hillside all opened before me. My thoughts relaxed from God and I could feel release even from the worries of the day, such as the question of who would speak at the lunch I was trying to organise. With these thoughts came quietness.

At the end of the walk, before taking the road back to Tremeirchion, I skirted the mountain of Ycrag and sat down there. This was a view unspoilt by the A55 road, or pylons, or even houses – just a mystical valley, cut into green stone-walled fields, spreading out into distant blue hills. It is easy enough to feel at peace in a spot like this. That night, I tried again an examination of conscience, looking into the good and the bad moments of the day, but in a place like this, it has to be said, nearly all the moments are good.

At the end of the second day, I was reading Margaret Hebblethwaite. She helped me a lot with one thing. I have always had difficulty in confession, because my sins, usually petty omissions, seem so trivial. What I should do, according to her, is to see my impulses, which I control, as the seed, or potentially the seed, of great evil in the world. I have no power over others, but sometimes I think "What if I did have power?" Before I could stop myself I might misuse that power, even hating some groups of people, and wishing to do them down in some way or another. Once or twice on a hot crowded London tube, I have had an insane impulse to hit someone (which of course, I don't). This is potentially the seed of all the violence and hatred in the world. Or I want to let someone down, but don't do it; but this is still the seed of betrayal and faithlessness.

All these impulses, and others in more difficult circumstances, have resulted in war, even genocide, adultery, murder ... they are all in me. If I had been in that situation, would I have given them free rein? Who knows? I fear I might. And that is my sin, and that is something worth being sorry for. I suppose Ignatius in his Exercises is trying to make one more open to understanding the source of sin.

Before going to bed on the evening of that second day, I sat in the lounge of the retreat centre. I needed some light relief. *The Irish RM,* an amusing novel about a nineteenth century rural magistrate in Ireland who is always getting into scrapes, was good because it did not invoke regret at not having persevered with a particular career, or invoke jealousy in my line of work. I also picked up a book of Monet's paintings. As usual, they filled me with pleasure and wonder – I was inspired but not at all jealous. How could I be? I love painting, but I know I cannot paint like that. However, I was inspired to go out and try again.

So I began to feel the same about people in my line of work – was I jealous of somebody's intelligence? I should just accept that he is cleverer than me. Was I jealous of someone's charm? They are simply more charming than me. Or jealous of someone's energy - they simply have more than me, and so on. One must just learn to accept things as they are, use them as an inspiration, and try to follow them as an example, but never to be jealous or resentful.

All these positive thoughts come so much easier if one is sitting in a quiet place trying to be guided by a Spiritual Director. How much more difficult in the real world! It must be a very intense experience doing a thirty day retreat, but all the more difficult to come out of it.

On the third day, Sister Helen explained to me the enneagram, a technique for analysing people's characters. She thinks St Ignatius is a 'Number 1', someone who always wants to do everything perfectly. The numbering seems to make sense to me. 'Number 1' are those who listen, who are leaders, organisers, and sometimes doers of little things, but little things done very well.

I explained to Sister Helen how my second day had gone. She rightly noted my mistake on the Colloquy of the first week, regarding the passage in The Spiritual Exercises, which says that "it is necessary to make ourselves indifferent to all created things in all that is allowed the choice of our free will, so that we want not health rather than sickness, riches rather than poverty, honour rather than dishonour, long rather than short life." As I was asked to do by the Exercises, I had talked to Jesus on the Cross, but I had asked wrongly what he could do for me in the afternoon. By the evening, I had realised that I should ask what I could do for him.

This led me into the second week of the thirty-day retreat advised by Ignatius. In that second week, one is supposed to ponder what one would do for a great temporal leader if asked to share his tasks and his table, and then ask one's self if one would make the same sacrifices for Christ. Most people, myself included, have to admit that they cannot or would not. So to help them, the Exercises lead them into a meditation on the life of Christ. One starts with the Incarnation.

Ignatius asks us to act out the scene of the Nativity visually, thinking of all the world, its beauty and its ugliness, going on its own way, and then God deciding to intervene decisively on its behalf. So, I sat down to read the Exercises for the second week, in order that I could be helped in understanding the process of loving Jesus, something I have always found very hard to do.

I always tried to remember to start each Exercise with prayerful recollection. By the early evening on the third day, I was starting to contemplate the call of Christ. I repeated the Colloquy to myself. Eventually I realised the implications. These were not just a few words to be rattled off: I was making a promise – "If you, my Lord and King, would so call and choose me, then take and receive me into such a way of life... To offer myself to you, to accept all poverty, actual and spiritual." But in truth, was I honest in promising this? Even if I did not have any children, I would have felt no great desire to renounce everything and go off to the slums of South America.

Equally, in one's ordinary life one cannot start talking about Jesus in every tenth sentence. People would think one a charlatan. Can I therefore just achieve what I have promised by being a better person? Many atheists are better and kinder, less selfish people than I am; therefore, what am I to do?

The only hope is to approach each day and each task according to whether it fits in more closely with what I imagine God wants. I know this getting closer to God makes me feel happier. Indeed, I know that I am happier on retreat as I do this more thoroughly, whereas, in normal life, perhaps a whole day will pass by while I think only of other things. But who is to be my guide?

I have had more difficulty with the idea of following Christ as God, than with simply believing in God. I accept the rational basis for the existence of God. Someone had to create the first matter; but Christ is more difficult. I realised that I often prayed to God rather than to Christ, but I began to think rationally about the matter. Would God just create a universe, as Monet constructed a beautiful picture, and leave it at that? The picture once painted is beautiful. Its blues and yellows will always make greens. Its browns won't conquer and destroy the light of the impression, but the universe is not a picture; it moves, it changes. God, rationally, must have intervened, but would he come down? Would he descend in a rocket and take over?

In that case, the universe would have ceased to have any free will, and *when* would he intervene? Would he intervene in a cave-man society, when there was no literature, and no memory? What would be the point? If he hadn't intervened, could he have allowed a kind of pagan world to develop nuclear weapons? No. Thinking about it entirely rationally, even without any element of faith, one has to come to the conclusion that 2000 years ago was the right time, and the decision to enter his creation as a man was the right way of going about things. How else could God justify his loving justice, except through the medium of Christ?

All this is, of course, eminently rational; but rationality is dry, lacking vision and inspiration. I now stop from time to time in the day, using the methods of Ignatius, to ponder and meditate.

I considered the Incarnation. The decision of Mary to accept her role as the Mother of God: she could have said "no". The whole breadth of the universe paused and, from this cosmic grandeur in my mind, I moved to a tiny part of one small world in an enormous universe, to a young girl being told of her destiny to save mankind. We are told of her choice. Of course, she wanted to serve God however she could, so her decision was never in doubt, but she did have a choice. I moved in my mind to the Nativity. I thought of the births that I had witnessed. Now I tried to deal with the picture with all five senses. I tried to smell, see, hear, touch, and taste the scene before me.

Then I started again, over and over again – the grandeur of the universal scene, the Annunciation (the appearance before Mary of the archangel Gabriel, telling her of her fate) and the Nativity, but still it fought within me as a rational historical event. I tried to dissolve scenes from reason into ever simpler thoughts and prayers, until the thoughts and prayers became shorter and shorter, almost breaths, or aspirations. Later that evening, I sat in front of the Blessed Sacrament in the chapel, knowing the desolation of dry and unanswered prayer. I tried the Jesus Prayer, saying the mantra over and over again: "Jesus have mercy on me, a sinner." I tried reflecting on Jesus' life, and then – inspiration came.

Why was I here? I reflected on Ignatius, on how he meditated at Loyola, at Aránzazu and at Montserrat; walking across the Roman Bridge at Manresa; sitting in the gorge alone above the Cardoner. As I did so, immediately, a great joy and sense of fulfilment lit up in me. I visualised his Manresa; the Seto cathedral; the streets; stuffy Barcelona on a hot day outside Isabelle Pasquel's home – and at last I started to relive his life in a real visual way. I even felt, perhaps, that he was talking to me, and I loved him, his haughty and childish chivalry and his enthusiasm. I loved him personally.

By late evening on the third day, I had struggled in vain all day to love Jesus. Apparently, that is often the result of the second week. It needs more time. Suddenly, Hebblethwaite gave me an insight, by suggesting that one looks at Ignatius' one-hundred-and-fourth exercise. I had copied it down and read it all day, but I had obviously not really understood it. The preliminary prayer of grace and the concluding Colloquy is an Ignatian method of prayer. I started by saying: "It will be to ask for an intimate knowledge of my Lord, who has become human for me, that I may love him more and more and follow him more closely, and in the Colloquy – according to the life I have received, I will beg for grace to imitate and follow more closely my Lord who has become human for me." I emphasised in my own mind the word "grace", and him becoming human for me, and I began to feel that that is the key.

On the fourth day of the retreat, I read through to Sister Helen my experiences of the third day. She too had been to Loyola and loved it. I was honest in explaining my difficulty in loving Jesus, rather than accepting God as a rational fact. She gave me clues as to how the Gospel could become more alive for me and more human. She advised me that I should approach the Gospels by asking for grace; that one should slowly read over a particular story. She gave me Mark 14, the feeding of the five thousand, and Peter attempting to walk on water to the boat where Jesus was. She asked me to read it quietly several times and then aloud to myself, and then to picture myself in a scene and to take part in it in a passive way, not to judge it or attempt to draw conclusions. She asked me to do this for half an hour, and then to pray and meditate about what it meant to me.

I asked her about the exercise of the "two standards" – where Ignatius compares good and evil, temporal and spiritual – and told her that, so far, all I had was Ignatius' image of Lucifer sitting on his throne with steam coming out of it and little devils running off in all directions, rather medieval imagery which means very little to a modern person. She explained that in this time of the retreat, people were asked to ponder the choices they have to make in life – to choose the life of the self, promoting oneself and gaining status through acquiring property or a good job; or alternatively, the way of poverty and simplicity. Not many people can choose poverty, certainly not absolute poverty, but people can choose a certain simplicity in their attitude to life.

During my talk my pager went off. I read it after the meeting. The message read, "During these sensitive times, colleagues should not talk to the media." What sensitive times? What had happened? I was agog to know.

I think it is good not to cut oneself off entirely during a retreat, because that way one remembers the pressures in daily life and the hopes and worries that tend to block off any kind (or most kinds) of spiritual feeling. In daily life, one's spiritual armour is tested with use. It is easy enough in a retreat. One is driving a comfortable spiritual car all alone down a wide empty road with an easy view and no traffic about, but in real life, one is driving one's little car, having to stop and start and dodge things all the time, with no time to admire the view.

I returned to the library, tried to calm myself down, and settled down to read Matthew 14. I don't know why, but, in considering my life, I thought what advice I would give to young people starting off on a career. I thought particularly of somebody starting off as a politician.

In that particular world, certainly, particularly if your party is in government, you have your hand on the tiller of the state, but there will be many other people with their hand on it as well. Most times, one doesn't have one's hand on the tiller at all; one is just a crewman standing on the forecastle shouting advice through the gale, or perhaps holding a rope a long way away from the helmsman. That's all useful; someone may hear; the sail may flap if one doesn't hold it in the right way – but it can all become dispiriting after about twenty years in the job, and perhaps this feeling of being dispirited eventually happens to everyone.

So, thinking about that, I felt that one needs to buttress one's life in any busy job with 'the four Fs' – faith, family, friends and finances.

First: faith. One must have a faith. For some that may be an interest in religion; for others, it may be in humanism; for others, some abiding enthusiasm which motivates their life and gives it a purpose. Again, for others, it might be a passion about a particular issue - it could be the third world or anything else. While for others it could be a hobby or a sport; an appreciation of music or art, but one must have some kind of faith, something to believe in.

Next: family. One should always stay with the family, be around them all the time. I read once that the former Prime Minister, Stanley Baldwin, only spent two nights away from his wife in some fifty years that they were married. We flit around so easily that that may be difficult nowadays, but it is an ideal.

Next: friends. I am perhaps weakest on this, but I have a few, even if they are mostly in my line of business. Always stick by them, that is the joy of friendship.

Finally, the fourth 'F': finances. Keep up your professional work, sometimes even when it loses interest or goes wrong, even if it earns very little, it's important to have something.

In the early evening on the fourth day, I had two Gospel readings to meditate on, Matthew 14:13-36 and John 13:1-17. I tried the method of thinking "just as if I was there." What struck me most about the feeding of the five thousand was that, after he had heard of the death of his friend John the Baptist, Jesus prayed, and prayed again after the feeding of the multitude. "What was he praying?" I wondered. It is this emphasis on his prayer that struck me more than the initial, more obvious thought, "Don't worry, God will provide." Or, "Don't worry, have faith, come to me, you can walk anywhere with faith."

On the fourth day, I walked up hill of Meanefa. It was a much shorter walk than usual. I stopped often and, on the way, went to the wrong chapel, where I thought again of the washing of the feet. Here, the question that struck me was, if I knew that tomorrow I was to be humiliated, beaten and put to death in a most painful way, would my first thought still be to wash the feet of my friends? I began to think how extraordinary this act was. Later in the chapel, thinking of these things, I closed my eyes after communion and was moved in a way I hadn't been before. I felt tears rolling through my closed eyes and falling on my clasped hands.

That afternoon, when I reached the summit I sat down. On the way up, I was thinking all the way of St Ignatius' two standards of Lucifer and Christ, and of the three ways of humility which he set down in the Exercises. At the top, it came to me that my life was, or had been, dysfunctional.

True, when, as a junior minister, I had been driven around I was quite happy to read the *Imitation of Christ* in the back of the car. True, I was happiest at Downside or Prinknash Abbey on retreat, but the feeling always faded. Really, I was like a drunk going twice a year to a health farm. Going to Mass, often every day, was not enough. I was easing my spiritual hangover from the self-indulgence of the day before.

I was not, in my ordinary life, taking all decisions – or perhaps any decisions – "to praise and serve God, not myself", as Ignatius asked me to do. Everywhere my agenda was myself. What would others think of me – would they think better of me if I said or did a certain thing? I realised that I could not follow the way of complete humility and of actual poverty.

St Ignatius, after getting his Master's Degree in Paris, didn't come home to a hero's welcome. Although he was ill, he went to a grim hostel for down-and-outs in his home town of Azpeitia. I could never do that – I like my comfort too much; but I came away with the conclusion that I could at least try to make more of an effort to do God's will and not my will. There again, it is difficult to know what God's will is, although the Bible surely provides some clues. Here, Gerard Hughes is helpful. Is what one is proposing to do merely to increase one's consolation of self and soul? One has to ask oneself whether one has a hidden agenda. All of this I thought as I walked down the hill.

By the fifth day of the retreat I was waking up with a slight feeling of depression, which apparently is perfectly normal. I made myself a cup of tea and wondered whether I should go for a run to shake myself out of it, but I just lay awake. I wondered to myself how I could serve God today, without making decisions, because, of course, there were none to make about ordinary life in the middle of a retreat.

Today, I was making my Confession. I thought of my guilt and my sin. Could I be honest in my confession about my whole life, in the way that St Ignatius had been totally honest about his whole life? His general confession, at Montserrat, lasted three days before he finally committed himself to a life as a poor pilgrim. I started thinking of my guilt and my sin all over again. I closed my eyes. Now, I saw it as a heaving red mass within me, stopping me from doing what was right. Then, I saw it as a huge boulder along the middle of a green path, and next, in trying to be honest, I saw it as a great black mess oozing out of me. I resolved to be honest, and as I ran, I cried.

That morning I talked to the Jesuit priest who had been sharing a cottage with me. He was travelling to London for a reunion with thirty of his friends who had joined the Jesuits with him forty years ago when he was eighteen. Seven were left in the Order.

I had my talk with Sister Helen. I talked of my experience of thinking through the washing of the feet. She said that at the end of our lives we seek to leave our most important message behind. From Jesus, the insight which came to me was simply one of service. It is strange how my insights occur from the simplest readings. I had not thought till she told me that God was using the five loaves and two fishes to show me that I can make do with resources, however slender.

I talked through the third and fourth week of the whole Spiritual Exercises, which I was trying to telescope into one week. She talked of the Passion of Jesus – his agony in the garden, humiliation under Pilate, crucifixion and death. She said that one does not necessarily have to live it oneself, but merely to observe it. Not as the disciples did, to run away from it, but, like the women, stay with the Passion and relate it to one's own life - whether bereavement, disappointment, loss of a job, or losing one's way in life. She then talked of the Resurrection. That realisation of hope, of a chink of light, doesn't come immediately. The disciples on the road to Emmaus did not immediately recognise Christ. Mary Magdalene thought him the gardener, but, eventually, consolation and light came.

Sister Helen then led me on to read Section 230 of the Spiritual Exercises, the *Contemplation of the Love of God,* which Ignatius wanted those who did his retreats to read on the way back home. She read me the prayer, which in the translation of David Fleming reads, "I beg for the gift of an intimate knowledge of all the goods which God lovingly shares with me. Filled with gratitude, I want to be empowered to respond just as totally in my love and service". If I live with someone, I want to share with them. I want to give as well as take. I determined to try and think on this theme today. For my prayer today, Sister wanted me to read John 21, where Jesus meets the disciples on the shore. She wanted me to think of myself as Peter, rushing forward to share a meal with him.

I talked of my Confession. I was surprised to hear that she goes only once or twice a year. She looks on Confession as a devotion and not an obligation. She told me that, to take part in Services of Reconciliation is a help if it is too much to go to Confession. She also told me, once I sat down it would be easy. She asked me to read the last two chapters of William Barry.

I started to make notes for the Confession. I read the passage in Hebblethwaite where she refers to St Ignatius' method of prayer in Section 238 of the Spiritual

Exercises. There is a reference there to the Seven Deadly Sins of Pride, Covetousness, Lust, Anger, Gluttony, Envy and Sloth. But what do these old terms mean to me? What am I proud about? What are my ambitions? What does sex mean to me? Have I shown anger? What am I dependent on with food or drink? Have I got professional jealousies? What am I lazy about? Do I direct love where I should?

Sister Helen carried on helping me by saying that I should talk, not so much about the daily examination of conscience, as a daily examination of consciousness. It is put well on page 144 of Hebblethwaite. She writes, "of the things I have done today, which do I now feel most happy about?" I will thank God for these times, and secondly, what do I now feel most discomfort about? I will ask for God's help to cope better with such situations in future, and, where fitting, I will say sorry.

On the evening of the fifth day of the retreat, I remembered that I had been debating earlier whether I would have to leave that day to get back for an appointment. I was also wondering if the day would throw up anything new. Well, it did; the fifth day, for me, had been a 'purgative' and a 'unitive' one, in Ignatian dialogue. This was a day in which one had purged oneself of guilt and thereby unified oneself closely to God. I described the feeling as a kind of black ooze seeping from me, a feeling that had dominated my day with increasing power.

Earlier, Sister Helen had taken me through a final reading of John, Chapter 21. This was the occasion when Jesus appeared to his disciples for the third time after his Resurrection. Peter answers the call and swims ashore. A charcoal fire awaits him and Jesus asks him three times if he loves him and then tells him to "tend my sheep". Sister Helen had hinted that the passage was heavy with symbolism.

I thought of my own life. Feelings of having achieved very little, like the fishermen fishing all night without catching any fish. Until someone called from the shore and said, "Throw the net out to starboard and you will find something", and a bumper catch comes in. There are so many analogies one can make with this fishing incident. About trying in vain to succeed at something on one's own and then finally succeeding with a little bit of help. Perhaps the fish just aren't there. Should one keep trying and cast the net in a different direction, or walk up and down the bank in search of them, or wait for the fish to return?

In that story, the fire on the shore, already burning for breakfast, makes a welcoming scene, something very homely. Around which the disciples were witnessing, according to the Church, the second person of the Blessed Trinity, both true God and true man, who had just risen from the dead to unlock the gates of heaven. I thought of the advice given by Christ, "if you really love me, feed my sheep."

Afterwards, I had read the passage in Luke of Christ asking for the cup to be taken from him during the Passion, but ready to drink it if it was his Father's will. I walked slowly to Tremeirchion and back by the way of the hills, and prayed again and again in the way that Ignatius advises one to do whilst contemplating a passage from the Scripture.

I stopped by a little mountain stream and, feeling the beginning of something new and helpful, "baptised" myself with a little water from it and walked on. I rehearsed the Seven Deadly Sins as they applied to me.

I saw all my petty sins of anger and envy, of pride, lust, gluttony, greed and sloth, which all might have become much more serious in different circumstances.

When I finally got to Confession the priest, of course, was kind, understanding, and helpful, before he spoke the words of absolution. We ended up talking about the little model in his garden of a Japanese Rock Garden. I came out elated. I walked up to the woodland chapel. That night I looked around at all the people having their dinner, most of them strangers to me. There had been very little conversation with them, but I saw them no longer as middle-aged people, I seemed to see through them, to their inner spirit, or rather the angels shining within them.

That evening I could read nothing. I just sat in front of the Blessed Sacrament, phoned home and came back to my room to write up these notes. I asked myself: could I find God in all things? Whatever situation we are faced with, however serious or trivial, tragic or comic, God is always there. Could I, like St Thérèse of Lisieux, find God in the simple act of picking up a speck of dust from the ground? This was like the favourite prayer of Ignatius. Could my prayer turn from head to heart, and could I live according to the true meaning of that prayer? That afternoon I turned round a fold of the hill and looked down upon the A55 leading out before me. I found it beautiful.

I had now come to my sixth and final day on the retreat, equivalent to the last few days of a thirty-day retreat. I went to have my last chat with Sister Helen. I talked of my experiences in reading through John 21, and how I felt that one was sometimes fishing, through no fault of one's own, where there were no fish. She gave me an insight as to why, in all his appearances after the Resurrection, Jesus was not recognised. Taken just as a story, that is difficult to understand, but we do not recognise him in our daily lives either. He is waiting on the shore with a charcoal fire and bread and fish, and we carry on fishing to no avail, ignoring him. Why do we not recognise him when, surely, it should be so easy to do so?

Sister Helen took me through the contemplation of the Exercises. It was a summary of all that I had tried to learn during my study. From the Exercises of the first week I had learned to praise God in everything. From those of the second, I looked at the Incarnation of God's presence in everything. From the third, I looked at the passion of God's labour in everything and, from the fourth, the resurrection and God's view of life in everything. She said that perhaps my calling was for God's love to flow through me to my children. All parents, faced with a teenage child who doesn't speak but just grunts, have a feeling of what God's life is like, with his rejected love. But, just as I love all my children, so God loves all of me.

Every day at the silent breakfast there was a Jesuit priest who was working for reconciliation in Portadown, Northern Ireland. On his last day, he talked me through his experiences and told me that alienation is greater now than it was twenty years ago, when he started his work. He spoke of how boys of one religion or another will not go into town in their school uniform to catch a bus back into the country for fear of being recognised. It was a depressing return to the problems of normal life, but my sense of being buoyed up was not really dented by one conversation about Northern Ireland.

There was a different atmosphere around the retreat house. It was a rest day in the thirty-day retreat. For the first time, people were talking over their coffee. Suddenly it was more like "real life". People were going off on day trips and I realised that I much preferred it to silence.

As I began to think of leaving, I was having depressing thoughts which were centred on myself, so I tried to get rid of them by thinking of other people and hoping that this would be a new start – no gimmicks in my job, just doing what people ask me to do, and helping people if I could. Also, trying to work on something not to impress other people, but doing it because it had to be done. I thought back to my last few moments on the retreat as I was preparing to leave.

Because it was a rest day, we had Mass in the woodland chapel at noon, just a dozen of us. We sat around Fr Tom, who faced us behind a small low table. I did the first and second readings about the feast of St Teresa of Avila. The response to the psalm was "Your words are truth", although I preferred the alternative response, 'The decrees of the Lord are truth and all of them just.' Perhaps Sister Helen asked me to do this reading because she had felt that my words were more than usually truthful in her last talk with me.

Then there was the passage in the Second Reading: "When we cannot choose words in order to pray properly, the spirit itself expresses our plea in a way that could never be put into words, and God knows everything in our hearts perfectly well". This seemed a fitting summary of something I had been taught on this retreat. It was a moving little service, as we passed the Host around and received communion together. Father Tom McGuinness gave me the name of a Jesuit Priest at Farm Street, the Jesuit HQ in London, to contact and another one in Brixton, something which I failed to follow up.

It was time to go. The train would be leaving in an hour-and-a-half. It was a time of waiting, of sitting for the last time in the library, in the lounge, of having some soup before going to the station. The taxi driver complained about a lack of business in Rhyll, and how I had been diddled by being made to pay £10.60 to get here on my journey out to the retreat. Did it really matter? No.

The train became increasingly crowded. I read in *The Times,* about Tory splits over Europe. The paper seemed obsessed with this subject. How many thousands of column inches had they devoted to it? But it didn't depress me. I tried to cheer myself up by reading a devotional book by St Robert Bellarmine, perhaps the greatest theologian of the Counter-Reformation, *Live Well, Die Holy.* I found it difficult to read and archaic. I felt unmoved.

Already, having left the retreat only a couple of hours before, a period of spiritual dryness was descending on me. The young man next to me was reading the business plan of an internet company. Wasn't there more to life than this, I wondered. Then I heard him have a positive conversation about publishing, and my mood improved. The train drew into Euston. The crowds of people were overwhelming and disorientating after seven days alone in a very quiet place. On the way home, I went for a walk to the Cathedral and prayed.

I came home. Some of the children even got up from *Neighbours* to kiss me. Even the one who didn't smile. Nicky hugged me. I was home. Natalia was away. Benny kissed me. Perhaps Sister Helen was right. Perhaps my calling is to love God through my children, or to pass the love of God to my children. I thought I should just write out a journal like this and pass it on to them.

On the seventh day after arriving home, I ended my notes on the retreat. It was already fading, and I had a sense of struggle to keep alive the spirit of it. I had to think for a moment what the reading for the Mass was today, and I couldn't remember what it was yesterday. I remembered that it was Teresa of Avila's feast day when I was still at St Beuno's, and that seemed to have more relevance to me than what I had heard back in the Cathedral at home on my return.

Today's reading was about "rendering to Caesar what is Caesar's", but it took a conscious effort, walking back through the park, to meditate upon it and draw the obvious conclusions, something that I had found so easy to do when I was on my retreat. In the reading, Jesus was refusing to make an extreme or simple answer to the Pharisees' question. My thoughts resonated with a row that had been going on all that week about some European problem. People were arguing whether too much power was going to Europe from the nation states, although I was blithely unaware of it during my retreat.

In Jesus' time people were arguing about a foreign, pagan power, namely Rome, which had taken too much power over the Jewish people. Jesus let it be. It would come to an end of its own accord. He concentrated on the essentials, on the world of the spirit. For me, the previous forty-eight hours since leaving the retreat had not been a complete regression. I even managed to take one of my daughters (and seven friends) to Spectrum Park, a hopelessly overcrowded leisure centre and swimming-pool, and still remain calm!

Later in the afternoon I went three times to see the final raising of the Ferris wheel, the millennium eye, in front of the Shell Centre. I remained perfectly tranquil throughout. It was delayed again and again, from 5pm to 8pm and then, finally, till after midnight. In the end, I stood there for four hours until 2.29am, when the engineer finally got called and it was raised, and the surviving twenty or so of us sent up a ragged cheer.

A daily and nightly examination of consciousness (following Sister Helen's approach) is proving useful. I try to think more of the good things than the bad things, the good thoughts more than the bad thoughts of the day. I attempt to keep in check creeping jealousy as I plough pointlessly through the pages of the Sunday newspapers. Talking to Fr Michael Seed always leaves me in a better mood. He has a certain aura of disengagement from the world that puts it into context. This was the reason I asked him to act as a sponsor for my son to go through secondary school.

Finally, to conclude my thoughts about the retreat, I remembered a story that had been told while on it, I think by a certain John Phillips. At one of his theology classes, there was a difficult atheist student, Tommy, who had long hair. He was always making loud sighs and irritating remarks. As he handed in his papers one day, he asked John if he would ever find God. The answer was: "No, you'll never find God, but God will find you." Later, John heard that Tommy had terminal cancer. Tommy went to see him, and John asked him, in a kindly way after a chat, "What did it feel like to have terminal cancer at the age of only twenty-four?" Tommy's answer was that it was better than being fifty and thinking only about business, booze and women. "I want to tell you something", said Tommy. "When I knew I had this illness I banged and banged on the bronze door of God and he never answered. Then, suddenly, I turned my back and he came in. I went to my father, who was reading a newspaper at the time, and I said, 'Dad I wanted to tell you something'. He looked up and moved the newspaper down three inches. I said to him, for the first time ever, 'I love you Dad'. Then he did something he had never done before, he cried, and he kissed me. I talked all night, with us holding hands. I believe God had moved me and him to come together."

Ever since that moment, I have always found that story inexpressibly moving, and I felt it was a good thought on which to end my attempts to understand the mind of St Ignatius, by doing a retreat in the way he had instructed. I now felt, not qualified exactly, but better equipped to try and understand more about his life as a pilgrim.

Meditation: Spiritual exercises

Prove me, O Lord, and try me; test my heart and my mind.
Psalm 26:2.
Let a man examine himself, and so eat of the bread and drink of the cup. I Corinthians 11:28.

I came to the monastery. Sitting in my room after tea, I read a leaflet on prayer. It gave a clue to remembrance: "ACTS" – the four parts of prayer: Adoration, Contrition, Thanksgiving, Supplication. Afterwards I went to Vespers and sat in the darkening church and walked around the grounds. Asking the usual question over again: why am I happy here?

At Vespers I took the wrong book down to the Abbey and couldn't follow the words. I had to sit back, let the psalms float over me and concentrate on the candle in the sacristy and the window of Christ and the Virgin Mary above it. I had a sharp stab of joy and happiness. I prayed. I directed my thoughts to God. I realized how little I do this. Why shouldn't I pray at home? Set up a candle and an icon in my bedroom or office. "Joy is in the contemplation of the Lord." The problem I have is with Resentment and Anger, caused often by feeling I am like an alcoholic who cannot be trusted with a single glass of wine. I must not read newspapers or care about what others are doing. "Do not compare yourself to others. There will always be greater or lesser than you. If you do, you will become arrogant or bitter." The words are those of St Ignatius.

Live in the pleasure of the moment. In what you are doing, live for the present.

Be happy with what you have got. Pray.

Chapter 2
The Spiritual Exercises and You

We can now look at Ignatius' masterpiece – The Spiritual Exercises. These were written by him in the 1520s, after his conversion experience. They are not meant to be read as a book. Indeed the language is somewhat archaic and difficult to read, but they are a wonderful treasure house of a spiritual guide. We must view them through the lens of Ignatius' love of the Gospels and see them as an attempt at a practical guide as to how to live out the Gospels. Ignatius wants us to imitate Christ. He wants us to be poor in heart, gentle in demeanour. He wants us to forget ourselves and to follow another: Christ. He wants us to use our new love, to spread it to all those we know and meet. He wants us to lose our need for possessions or labels. He wants us to be mocked if necessary. He wants us, in short, to do two things: to love God and to love each other.

So what does this book mean to you? You accept that you have a yearning for something spiritual. Sometimes you manage to take yourself – your very self – out of the churning worries of your day-to-day mind, but you need some help. Church doesn't seem to do much for you. It is a jumble of ancient words. It will help in time, but not yet. On your own you can make a certain amount of progress, then, quickly you hit a plateau. This is where The Spiritual Exercises may come in useful.

There is nothing obligatory about them. They are only a tool. There are many others. They are designed merely to help you to pray. Remember this. The language, the story, is not in itself so important, what is important is finding something to help us pray, to get us out of this world and to find a new, better life. Each part is based around a passage from the Gospels. What you should get out of each passage is not set out. It is for you to decide what the Gospel passage means for you but, to help you, from time to time Ignatius gives meditations to dwell on.

The idea is that, over a four week period, you do the Exercises with a Spiritual Director at a retreat house, in an atmosphere of complete calm and silence. This is of course impossible for most of us, but Ignatius himself envisaged busy people attempting them in the midst of a busy life. There are people better qualified than myself who can give good advice on the Exercises, notably, extremely well-trained Jesuit priests. I myself am indebted to the late Michael Ivens SJ, and many others, including the staff at St Beuno's Retreat House. It may be that an untutored layman like me may have a few useful insights, precisely because I've got a questioning nature. Anyway here goes!

* * * * *

The Exercises are centred on the life of Jesus. So, first, ignore any doubts or questions you may have about whether Jesus is God. We all have those. Just assume it to be the case for the present, for the sake of argument if you like. I promise you, if you concentrate on his life, then, like St Ignatius, a feeling of contentment will surround you. Whereas reading novels, watching television or glancing at tabloid newspapers – while enjoyable at the moment – may leave you with a feeling of dissatisfaction at the end.

Now try some of these Exercises. Think of St Ignatius' Principles and Foundation:

> "The human person is created to praise, reverence and serve God Our Lord, and by so doing save his or her soul…"

In other words, we are not here just to pass through a daily grind of household and work-related chores. We are not here to acquire possessions. We are not here either just to pursue higher destinies, becoming proficient in a trade or a profession, or being part of a family – important as all these things are. We are here for one ultimate purpose: *to save our eternal souls*. Let that amazing fact sink in for a while. That is a truly inspirational aim for our lives.

Ignatius goes on to say:

> "…and it is for the human person that the other things on the face of the earth are created, as helps to the pursuit of this end. It follows from this that the person has to use these things in so far as they help towards this end, and to be free of them in so far as they stand in the way of it."

We might think and ponder for a moment here. Everything that we see about us, all that we touch, see, hear and feel is real, certainly, but not an *ultimate* reality. This is one reason why the Jesuits had *trompe l'oeil* (deceive the eye) designs put into their churches, to demonstrate that the senses can deceive – but also that they can be used to lead us closer to the ultimate reality.

Of course, eventually the world of sense-impressions will all pass away, and before very long our bodies will pass away from it.

This beautiful tree will wither and die, and even before that happens, so will we. We can all accept that, but more important, all these 'things' are created for a purpose – to help me on my way. They are the means to the end, not the end itself.

If this book helps you towards finding your soul, use it. If anything – a church service, an empty church, a quiet room – helps you, use it. If all your many possessions hinder you, you may not be able to discard them. Don't worry! Very few of us are monks or hermits, or want to be, but put your possessions into perspective. In themselves they are not important.

The last section of St Ignatius' Principles and Foundation tells us:

> "To attain this, we need to make ourselves indifferent towards all created things, provided the matter is subject to our free choice and there is no prohibition. Thus for our part we should not want health more than sickness, wealth more than poverty, fame more than disgrace, a long life more than a short one – and so with everything else; desiring and choosing only what conduces more to the end for which we are created."

This paragraph is the distilled essence of Ignatius' thought. We will only make progress towards our aim of accessing a deeper spiritual life and finding true happiness to the extent that we make ourselves indifferent to created things. We can possess them, we can use them, we can enjoy them, but we almost have to learn to laugh at them, to handle them for the present, enjoying them, realising they have little importance for the future. Even something as "important" as having a long rather than a short life. Even something as vital to my self-esteem as how other people view me. Even good health rather than bad health. Even a comfortable lifestyle, rather than being unemployed or on benefit. None of these things is really of fundamental importance. Indeed they merge into a mist, in the phrase of the anonymous mediaeval English mystic, a "cloud of unknowing" that blinds me to my true vocation.

We can now pass to the daily and weekly Exercises, remembering always that St Ignatius envisaged that we would not do these on our own but with the help of a Spiritual Director. You may be shy at doing this at first, but think about it. In time you may pluck up courage to go along to your nearest church and get help.

St Ignatius also planned for you to take time off for thirty days. For most, this is probably impossible, but he also, in his famous nineteenth annotation, envisaged a retreat in daily life for busy people. So this is the framework of how you might proceed.

Ignatius divided up his Exercises into four weeks, but you can do them as you wish. First, he advises a Particular and General Examination of Conscience. He suggests a particular examination of conscience three times a day, "The first time in the morning. Upon arising, the retreatant (the one who meditates) should resolve to guard carefully against the particular sin or fault he wants to correct or amend." This is, in any event, a good and useful thing to do. Waking can be a depressing experience. Quite apart from the unpleasant physical prospect of getting up, there are the depressing worries that come into the mind as it considers the day in prospect.

So use Ignatius' technique. Dedicate your day to God and ask for help in your good resolution.

"Before the noon meal", Ignatius advises that, "the 'exercitant' (the person taking the retreat), should ask God Our Lord for what he desires, namely grace to recall how often one has fallen into the particular sin or fault in order to correct it in the future." This is good discipline. but Ignatius gives a rather burdensome instruction that one should write down all these faults in an exercise book. This may be too much to ask for! Ignatius then advises that we should repeat the exercise at supper.

The Spiritual Exercises are difficult to read. The language is old-fashioned. It cannot be stressed too much that they are much more effective if done with help, but with the right sort of modernised interpretation, they provide a useful basis for daily meditation on one's own.

Ignatius then passes on to a general examination of conscience "to purify oneself and to make a better Confession." He sees thoughts as coming from good or evil forces outside. He thinks that daily life is a constant struggle to resist "evil thoughts" as they come into the mind. Can we stand apart from our thoughts, analyse them and accept or reject them according to whether they sit squarely with a good conscience?

The Exercises start with the "Annotations". These are just notes to give guidance to the retreat provider and the retreatant or exercitant.

The First Annotation

Let us look at the First Annotation.

> "The term Spiritual Exercises denotes every way of examining one's conscience, of meditating, contemplating, of praying vocally and mentally

and other spiritual activities as will be explained later. For just as strolling, walking and running are exercises for the body, so 'spiritual exercises' is the name given to every way of preparing and making ourselves ready to get rid of all disordered affections so that, once rid of them, one might seek and find the divine will in regard to the disposition of one's life for the salvation of the soul."

I can see you already telling yourself that this all sounds rather old fashioned, even pompous. For instance what is a 'disordered affection'? Let's try and explain it.

My youngest son loves swimming. He came back after a training session absolutely exhausted. Probably in the hour he was plying up and down the pool he had actually, despite all this effort, made an imperceptible improvement to his technique. Trying to get more into understanding religion is like that. True, some people are lucky. For them, religion is always there, or it comes to them in a flash of inspiration. Personally, I'm much more of a plodding long distance swimmer, as, I think, are most of us. I believe that you just have to persevere with daily reading, prayer and church attendance without making too much demand on belief. Then, very slowly, religious exercises become so much a part of one's life, a pleasurable part, that, like the regular jogger, you don't want to give them up. This doesn't mean it is necessarily all true, even more than jogging is true or false, it just is.

My other son comes home with his GCSE textbook on Theology. It is full of the most complicated arguments about proofs and dis-proofs of God, such as St Thomas Aquinas' argument that everything needs a 'first mover'. But to me the most interesting "proof" of the existence of God lies in the "numinous" experience that people have, a feeling that they can't account for, but that something else is out there. This is where St Ignatius' 'disordered affections' come in.

In the sixth century BC the Buddha realised our life was blighted by affections or feelings: our fear of death, disease or poverty. The purpose of these Spiritual Exercises is – gradually, over many weeks – to reorder our priorities, so that step-by-step the spirit enters into our thoughts.

One way of understanding this at a deeper inspirational level might be to reflect on the day's readings. As I write this, it is the Feast of the Exaltation of the Cross and I listened to the wonderful passage from St John, where he talks about Nicodemus.

God so loved the world that he gave his only son to save it. As I laid awake in the night I concentrated on an image of a relic of the True Cross that had been shown to us in Westminster Cathedral. "Obviously a fake", the sceptic will scorn, but it is like when we admire the rebuilt Cutty Sark – maybe not much of its original wood survives, but its essence or spirit carries on, as does that of the relic. The image of the relic became suffused in light – this was not a dream or a vision, something much more prosaic. Just an image implanted on the retina, but a good thing to fall asleep with!

The Second Annotation

In his Second Annotation St Ignatius writes,

> "For it is not so much knowledge but the inner freeing and relish of things that fills and satisfies the soul."

This is the key point. In order to do something effectively we often have to let go of the conscious rational process. This does not mean that knowledge is necessarily a bad thing, indeed a foundation is essential, but it will only get us so far.

All the commentaries that I have ever read on the Exercises are written by Jesuit priests. They have obviously come to the conscious decision to believe that the Gospels are the work of an existing God. This is fine, but I am more interested in writing for those who struggle with belief. There is a good book entitled, *Drawing on the Right Side of the Brain*. Its author, Betty Edwards, argues that at around about the age of eleven, children lose their self-confidence to draw and adults rarely regain this confidence because the rational side of the brain intervenes and destroys their self-confidence. I believe that the religious non-experience of most adults in the West is like this. We need to suspend knowledge for a time and release our inner feeling.

The Third Annotation

> "Throughout the following spiritual exercises we make use of the understanding in order to think things over, and of the will in order to rouse the affections. We should therefore note that in the activity of the will when we speak vocally or mentally with God our Lord or with his saints, greater reverence is required on our part than when we use the intellect to understand."

Knowledge is the building block but, in releasing the will or the heart, we can slowly free ourselves of those worldly affections and allow ourselves to approach a God who is necessarily not of this world, but transcendent. It is clear that here Ignatius is saying that, when we start to pray, greater reverence is needed.

When we start something like the Exercises, the novelty of the thing, and of the topics to be discussed, may be more interesting than prayer.

Andre Ravier SJ, in his book *A Do It At Home Retreat*, says that we should use the opportunity at the start of the Exercises to put all our effort into finding what we are looking for at the particular stage of the retreat where we are. This must be good advice, as he goes on to say, "If by chance we have an inordinate attachment or inclination toward something or someone, it is very good to go against and exercise all our force in opposition to what we find is improperly so attractive."

Thus, as I was writing this, I got ridiculously angry about a chore I had to do. In realising the stupidity of my thoughts, I think the Exercises were telling me to fight against my propensity to put my own comfort first.

Annotations 4-20

With regard to the first four of these Annotations, we do not need to go into these in any great detail as they are written for Retreat Directors. The fourth annotation tells us that the Exercises are designed to last four weeks. The first is for the "consideration and contemplation of sins". The second, for looking at the "life of Christ our Lord, up to and including Palm Sunday." The third looks at the Passion of Christ and the fourth considers the Resurrection and Ascension, together with three ways of praying.

All these we can look at later, but it is good to think about what we are letting ourselves in for. Of course, all timings and progress will be up to us! As Ignatius himself tells us, "it may be necessary sometimes to shorten the week and at other times to extend it."

In the fifth Annotation we are asked to begin the Exercises, "In a magnanimous spirit and with great liberality to our Creator and Lord", and to offer him all our powers of desire and all our liberty. I believe this is the essential point of the Exercises. Later on we will think upon Ignatius' "Principle and Foundation", his great statement about the need to put God at the centre of all things, but at this stage we are only asked to approach the Exercises with an open heart.

From the sixth to the eleventh Annotations the Retreat Director is given practical advice as to what to do when we the retreatant moves between too much enthusiasm and too much apathy! The advice is obvious – take it slowly and be understanding.

The twelfth and thirteenth Annotations deal with the amount of time we are to spend on the Exercises. I don't want to put you off, but the specified time is an hour each day on each of the five daily exercises. Let us leave this to the very few people who will have the time or inclination to take themselves off to a retreat house for thirty days, ours is a more modest endeavour.

The fourteenth and fifteenth Annotations were written for people who are so overcome that they decide to follow a religious calling or embrace poverty. That is unlikely to happen to us, so we can move on.

The sixteenth Annotation can apply to all of us, "If the soul in question happens to be attached or inclined to something in an ill ordered way, it is very useful for him to do all in his power to bring himself round to the contrary of that wrong attachment." What I think we are being called to do is to move away from putting ourselves, our comfort and ambitions and our fears at the centre of everything. Ultimately this does not mean

181

endless, tedious self-denial, but a route to true freedom from the chains that bind us to the world. Happiness is what we hope for.

When Ignatius talks of "Wrong attachments" what he means is "For example, if a person were bent on seeking an appointment not for the honour and glory of God, nor the spiritual good of others, but for one's own advancement and temporal interests." Of course he is thinking here primarily of clergymen, but this can equally apply to us. We can never get away entirely from these personal attachments, what Ignatius calls the "first attachment", unless we are saints, (which we decidedly are not) but we can start making progress along the road, one step at a time.

In the seventeenth Annotation Ignatius talks about the value of openness with the retreat giver. Whilst it may be difficult in a busy life to have a regular Spiritual Director, and often more so to find one who is genuine friend and soul-mate, it is enormously valuable and worth searching for.

In the eighteenth Annotation Ignatius makes the obvious point that, "The Exercises are to be adapted to the capabilities of those who wish to engage in them; that is to say age, education or intelligence are to be taken into consideration." In other words, we can do everything at our own pace! Thank God.

We now come to the famous nineteenth Annotation, which is about us. "A person taken up with public affairs or necessary business, and who is educated or intelligent, can set aside for the Exercises an hour and a half a day". In our age of short attention spans, this seems a lot. However, let us not get too hung up on it, but don't give up on it either. The important thing is that we can attempt this in the midst of our ordinary life.

The twentieth and last Annotation is for those who want to attend the whole course in seclusion. Now we start on the four-week long Exercises.

THE FIRST WEEK

Principle and Foundation

In this section St Ignatius outlines the core of the Exercises.

> "The human person is created to praise, reverence and serve God our Lord, and by so doing save his or her soul; and it is for the human person that the other things on the face of the earth are created, as helps to the pursuit of this end."

It follows that the person has to use these things in so far as they help towards this end, and to be free of them in so far as they stand in the way.

> "To attain this, we need to make ourselves indifferent towards all created things, provided the matter is subject to our free choice and there is no prohibition. Thus for our part we should not want health more than sickness, wealth more than poverty, fame more than disgrace, a long life more than a short one – and so with everything else; desiring and choosing only what conduces more to the end for which we are created."

What we are being asked to do here is not to leave what we have to do in our jobs or our homes, I think, but to have a life that circulates around God rather than ourselves. Easily said, but very difficult to achieve. Even more difficult is his injunction not to worry about a successful life or even a long life, but again to put our relationship with God first. The length of our life is one of the principal components of our own sense of worth. How could it be otherwise?

Yesterday, I went to sit beside an old friend and his family as he lay dying of a relentless disease. At the end, he slipped away so gently that it was barely noticeable. A beautiful and peaceful death, a gentle slowing down and quietening of the breathing, a slight flutter of breath as gentle as the flight of a butterfly and he was gone. Where to, none of us can ever know. My friend was not religious but one of the last things he said to me was that all this cannot be for nothing, that there must be some survival of the consciousness somewhere.

I believe that Ignatius' difficult Principle and Foundation becomes easier to achieve if we accept that we are not alone. That, although we are absolutely unique, we also share something with every other person who has been and will be. That we have two natures. Just as we want to believe that Christ had two natures, human and divine, so we are all temporary and human, as well as permanent and divine in a way we cannot fathom.

The Foundation is an Exercise on its own and we could spend several days meditating on it. It may have been published as long ago as 1548, but it is profound and surprisingly modern. Looking at it more closely, it is written on two levels – the general and the personal. It should also be read in the context of the fifth Annotation, which we have already looked at, in other words, in a spirit of open mindedness. This does not mean that we have to be "indifferent" now "to all created things". It would be good to want this or strive for it or even (and this is only my reaction as a lay-man), to realise that this indifference may only come at the end of life, a kind of "make me holy but not yet" syndrome, but it should be there in some form.

Indifference can also suddenly hit us with regard to religion. One day I was in Walsingham, and at the start of Mass, everything seemed wrong, even ridiculous and rather mumbo jumbo-ish. It was only after a passage from St Thérèse of Lisieux was read out that I warmed to the whole thing. She wrote, "I had discovered where it is that I belong in the Church, the niche God has appointed for me. To be nothing else than love, deep down in the heart of Mother Church". After Mass, I sat alone in the tiny Slipper Chapel and felt profoundly moved as I looked at the green folds of the altar covering moving in the reflected light. Indifference had given way to acceptance in a little over an hour. But then again, I was in Walsingham.

The more you read the Foundation the more you can get out of it. For instance, in talking of all things that are created, Ignatius could be expressing the idea of the unity of all things and that all things are part of a beautiful temple of God.

Confession

Ignatius imagines the retreatant making a "general" confession, that is to say, a confession of all the sins of one's life so far. Many people find going to Confession one of the most difficult things to do and I am no exception, so I would never lecture anyone about it. Too often it can be just a dreary repetition of the same innocuous "sins", for fear of letting on about the more embarrassing ones.

I think it is better to go to Confession and mention the easy ones and seek help to not skirt around those of a more difficult nature, than to not go to Confession at all. There is something wonderfully soothing about the priest's absolution, however mumbling and pathetic the Confession. In any event, the best Confessions are often those made on retreat for, in that context, one's inhibitions about confronting the truth break down.

Ignatius asks us to concentrate on our thoughts, words and deeds. This is obviously a first step, but he also wants us to keep a little notebook to remind us day by day when we have fallen short. He marks each line with a "G" – perhaps this stands for Giorno, the Italian for day. Frankly, this is too much for me, but when I was thinking of his advice, lying half-awake in the night, I felt a great feeling of goodwill towards everyone and everything, so I'm sure his method works. Of course, the next morning, I immediately felt angry about something and I had to start again, but this is the point of these Exercises!

Making the general examen

There are five steps in making a general examen (self-reflection) and they can be a constant of prayer. In the first instance, "to give thanks to God for the benefits I have received"; secondly, to "ask for grace to know my sins and reject them"; thirdly "to ask an account of my soul… with regard to thoughts, then words and finally deeds"; fourthly "to ask for pardon for my sins" and finally, the fifth, "to resolve to amend with his grace".

We should pause, particularly on the first of these, because as we do so we are with Ignatius in seeing God at the heart of all things. As I write this I am staring out at the magnificent cliffs and a bright blue sea on a sunny day in North Cornwall where, with my wife, we have come to celebrate our twenty-fifth wedding anniversary. It is easy to see God in all things when looking at Pentire Point in Cornwall, more difficult in the three mile traffic jam on the M5 getting here, and there's the rub!

Ignatius wants us to make a regular examination of our conscience every day while we attempt his Spiritual Exercises. He starts with what he calls "The particular examen". It makes a good start to the meditations of the first week, but is also a useful tool at any time. What he suggests is that three times a day – upon rising, after lunch and after dinner – we examine our conscience

"The first time is in the morning immediately on rising; the exercitant should make a firm resolve to take great care to avoid the particular sin or defect that he or she desires to correct and amend."

"The second time comes after the midday meal, when one should ask God our Lord for what one desires, namely: the grace to remember how many times one has fallen into that particular sin or defect, and to amend for the future".

We then repeat the process in the evening.

It is important that we do not just focus on negative parts of our behaviour, but try also to develop our positive side as well.

Five meditations
First meditation

The point of the first "week" is to purge your soul of all the wreckage that clogs it up. By freeing the soul of doubt and sin we can make better progress towards God. During all these Exercises, Ignatius asks us to imagine ourselves in the gospels, to try and actually "see" them with one's mind's eye:

"It should be noted here that for contemplation or meditation about visible things, for example, a contemplation on Christ our Lord (who is visible), the 'composition' will consist in seeing through the gaze of the imagination the material place where the object I want to contemplate is situated. By 'material' place I mean for example a temple or a mountain where Jesus Christ or our Lady is to be found – according to what I want to contemplate."

As well as putting ourselves in the place where the gospel scene is taking place, Ignatius asks us in a "prelude" to the contemplation to request the feeling appropriate to the subject of each contemplation, in empathy with Christ. Or, in his words, to "ask God our Lord for what I wish for and desire… in contemplating the Resurrection, one asks for joy with Christ joyful, while in contemplating the Passion one asks for grief, tears and great suffering with Christ suffering." Of course, in the purgative way, in this very first meditation, Ignatius wants us to ask for "shame and confusion about myself."

The first biblical scene one can imagine, suggests Ignatius, is the fall of the rebel angels, and how for one sin they were "banished to hell" for ever. "For one sin they went to hell… how often have I deserved hell for my many sins", writes Ignatius. He also wants us to think of the angels "created in grace, and then not wanting to better themselves by using their freedom to reverence and obey their creator and Lord. They fell into pride, were changed from grace to malice and were hurled from heaven into hell."

The important thing is that Ignatius wants us to run this round and round in our mind, to "ruminate" on it with the "intellect", and then "move yourself to deeper emotions by means of your will." This is supposed to be a deeply stirring, emotional experience. We will start to feel regret, even shame, about our lives and ourselves, but remember, out of this cleansing fire will come resurrection, new hope and new life.

Ignatius then asks us to think on the original sin of Adam and Eve, of how they were "placed in the earthly paradise" and how, after eating the "forbidden fruit of knowledge", they were expelled from paradise, and lived out their whole lives in hardship and penance. In a colloquy, Ignatius asks us to "imagine Christ your Lord, suspended on the cross before you." We must then converse with him. This is important. Ignatius wants us to be physically with Christ in this world, and converse with him. We must ask him directly: What have I done for Christ? What am I doing for Christ? What ought I do for Christ? All of this as we gaze on him "in his pitiful state." This is essential. For too many of us, the Passion is akin to an academic exercise. We do not live it as if we were there, witnessing the horror of the nails being driven into living flesh.

I recently went to an open-air play, where the Crucifixion was acted out before my eyes. It brought the scene home to me in a way that countless readings had not. The same would have been true for people in medieval times, who regularly saw Passion plays acted out by members of trade guilds on a simple wooden stage. In fact, it is certain, according to the historian Eamon Duffy in his book *The Stripping of the Altars,* that they knew the Gospel story better, in that illiterate age, than the majority of people living now. One could easily – if that is the right word – have a similarly powerful experience by watching Mel Gibson's film *The Passion of the Christ* on DVD. St Ignatius would have approved of it most warmly.

Second meditation

Ignatius now asks us to look at all the sins of our life, "year to year or from one period to another." We must think of where we were living and what our job was at the time. The language is strong and seldom heard nowadays: "foulness of malice of each deadly sin."

We should compare your own sins to others' and to those of perfect entities such as angels. Does Ignatius ask too much of us? "I will look at myself as though I were a running sore, from which many sins and evils have flowed, and the most vile poison." He feels that welling up within us should be "an exclamation of wonder and surging emotion."

As I think of the glories of nature, "The heavens, the sun, the moon, the stars, and the elements, the fruits, the birds, the fishes and the animals, how have they kept me alive until now? As for the earth, how has it not opened to engulf me, creating new hells where I might suffer for ever?"

One should conclude the second exercise with a "colloquy of mercy", thanking God for one's life up to the present and planning to reform it in the future. A colloquy is a kind of talk with God.

Third meditation

In the third Exercise we repeat the first and second Exercises, dwelling upon "the points where I felt greater consolation or desolation, or greater spiritual relish."

Ignatius invokes the help of the Virgin Mary, so that I may feel an "interior knowledge of my sins and an abhorrence for them" and the help of Jesus Christ and the Father.

Fourth meditation

This is a repetition of the third.

Fifth meditation

Ignatius asks us to imagine hell:

> "The great flames and… souls as though in bodies of fire… the waillings, howls, cries… smoke, sulphur, filth and putrefaction."

The modern mind will find all this very difficult. The truth is that few people believe in hell, but there is always a choice, an alternative. Can I not choose to reject God? How can he deny me that rejection? To do so would be to impose on my free will and would remove all virtue from the fact of my 'loving' Him. You cannot, by definition, force someone to love you. In any event it is useful to imagine hell, not just through a dry sense of the intellect, but also to try and see it, smell it, touch it and taste it, and think of those who are actually in hell because of their lifetime choices.

In additional directives, Ignatius gives advice to aid meditation and concentration, such as thinking when going to bed about the Exercises you are to do the next day. He suggests pausing for a moment before starting an exercise, and imagining Our Lord looking down upon oneself, and concentrating in this week, not on the glories and hope of the Resurrection, but upon "pain, sorrow and tears." He also advises penances, such as forswearing superfluous food and sleep.

The modern person will not want to accept his option of hurting oneself with tight cords, but such self-imposed physical mortifications were practised by the vast number of the saints, including Francis of Assisi,

Thomas More, John Fisher, Philip Neri and Josemaria Escriva, so we at least have a good pedigree. However, this is not to suggest that anyone should be tempted to make use of any physical mortification, other than the regular rules of fasting and abstinence.

At the end of the first week we are asked to consider Ignatius's "Additions". We do not need to take these too literally. For instance he states: "The fourth addition. I will enter upon the contemplation, now kneeling, now lying on the ground prostrate or face upwards, now seated, now standing, but always intent on the search for what I want." This may be a bit over the top, but the point of what we are being asked to consider is what works for us. How can we pray more effectively?

Thus:

> "The fifth addition. After finishing the exercise I will either sit down or walk around for a quarter of an hour while I see how things have gone for me during the contemplation or meditation. If badly, I will look for the cause, and having found it, I will be sorry, in order to do better in the future… and if well, I will thank God our Lord and proceed in the same way another time."

THE SECOND WEEK
OVERVIEW AND CALL OF THE TEMPORAL KING

We now move to the second week. We call it a week, but it may be shorter or longer. The first week was a kind of self-expurgation. During the second week we seek a deeper spirituality through pondering the life of Christ.

Ignatius thinks that during this and the following weeks it is profitable to read through either Thomas á Kempis' *Imitation of Christ*, the gospels, or some lives of the saints. The *Imitation* has inspired generations of Christians. It always seems particularly valuable during retreats, because it gently leads one into a frame of mind of rejecting the crushing, clanging values of the day-to-day world.

In this week too we will come to the Election. We elect to gain in Christ. We are to discover that our own personal experiences arise from our contemplation of the life of Christ. First we have a prayer. "The first prelude: is the composition, made by seeing the place. Here it will consist in seeing with the eyes of the imagination the synagogues, towns and villages where Christ our Lord went preaching."

"The second prelude: to ask for the grace I want. Here it will be to beg our Lord for grace not to be deaf to his call, but alert to fulfil his most holy will to the best of my ability."

To end our meditation, Ignatius imagines us standing before a king. The modern mind may not see a "king" as the supreme role-model. If so, choose another role-model. The point is to imagine someone you may admire and follow and then to compare them to Christ who deserves even more commitment. "The first point is to put before myself a human king chosen by the hand of God our Lord, to whom all Christian leaders and people pay homage and obedience."

Regarding the first point, if such a call made by an earthly king to his subjects claims our consideration, how much more is it worthy of consideration to see Christ our Lord, the eternal King, with the entire human race before him, calling to each of us:

"My resolute wish and desire and my considered determination – on the sole condition that this be for your greater service and praise – is to imitate you in enduring every kind of insult and abuse, and utter poverty both actual and spiritual, if your most holy majesty wishes to choose me and receive me into that life and state."

This seems to me to be a central point of the exercises. We are asked to elect to give ourselves to Christ, in whatever state we find ourselves.

The first day

Once again we imagine with our senses and not just our intellect. We imagine the world going about its business, happy and sad people, people at peace and at war, healthy and sick people, people being born and dying – the whole great mass of humanity in all its diversity. We imagine the divine persons looking down on all this and saying, "Let us bring about the redemption of the human race."

Then listen to the angel coming to Our Lady and informing her of her destiny and what it means to us. Then, in a second contemplation, imagine and visualise the pregnancy of Our Lady, and the journey to Bethlehem. We should consider the road's length and breadth; whether it is level or winds through valleys and hills. Similarly, look at the place of the Nativity: How big is it, or small? How low or high? And how is it furnished? After the birth we see Our Lady and Joseph, the maidservant and the infant Jesus after his birth. You will make yourself a poor, little and unworthy slave, gazing at them contemplating them and seeing them in their needs, just as if you were there.

Next, reflect on all this, how all this journeying has taken place, so that the saviour of the world can be born in utter poverty, only to die on the cross, and all this for us.

Then in a Third and Fourth Contemplation, repeat the first two.

In a Fifth Contemplation apply the five senses to all this. In an intimate way, listen to what Mary says; smell the fragrance of divinity; with our sense of touch, kiss and embrace the places where these people have walked or sat.

The second day

The exercitant should take as the subject of his First and Second Contemplations, the Presentation in the Temple (Luke 2:22-39) and the Flight into Egypt (Matthew: 2:13-18).

These exercises follow the Joyful Mysteries of the Rosary. First, The Annunciation, then The Visitation, The Nativity, The Presentation in the Temple and finally The Finding of Jesus in the Temple. The Rosary has a bad reputation amongst non-Catholics, that of twitching of beads and a false piety, but, like these exercises, it is a marvellous aid to meditation. As one says the ten Hail Mary's for each subject one can imagine and see in the mind's eye, as St Ignatius wants us to, the scenes of Jesus' life as they unfold in front of us. For instance, the scene of The Presentation in the Temple is particularly beautiful because it introduces to us the *Nunc dimittis,* as Simeon says, "Lord, now lettest thou thy servant depart in peace, according to thy word: for mine eyes have seen thy salvation, which thou hast prepared before the face of all people."

The third day

The exercise should be repeated as before, contemplating "how the child Jesus was obedient to his parents at Nazareth, and how afterwards they found him in the Temple;" again using all the senses as before.

We need to ask for grace from Our Lord and Our Lady to help achieve a receptive state of mind.

The fourth day

Ignatius wants us to see our life as a constant battle between Christ calling us to come to his standard, and Lucifer to his. He actually imagines the Devil on a throne of fire and smoke, sending his associates to different parts of the world to subvert people. He thinks of the Devil as a military leader,

> "An officer in command of an army takes up a position, makes a reconnaissance... and launches an attack at the weakest point. Similarly, the enemy of our human nature where he finds us weakest and most defective – he attacks at that point, seeking to overthrow us."

The imagery seems archaic, scarcely believable, but it illuminates in a powerfully visual way the real presence and threat of evil. We know how that in our lives our worst impulses always seem most unbearable and ready to overcome us.

We are to imagine the Devil trapping people with "chains and snares, coveting riches in order to obtain honour" and "passing to surging pride" and finally, being enticed to all the other vices. Christ, meanwhile, is sending out his army, encouraging people to crave for spiritual and actual poverty, welcoming reproaches and contempt, and thus acquiring humility.

Ignatius asks us to make a meditation on the three classes of persons who are each given a very large sum of money (a few thousand ducats). The first makes no effort at all to get rid of it, although he feels he should. The second class of person would like to get rid of attachment to the money, whilst actually keeping it. The third class of person also wishes to get rid of the money and is prepared to do so simply according to what they think is better for the "service of praise of the Divine Majesty."

This meditation, like the one on the two standards, is designed to lead us to a burning desire for actual poverty. In this second week, we now come to St Ignatius' famous "election" between the States of Life. What sort of life does Our Lord want us to follow? How are we to "come to perfection?"

The fifth day

We are to think of Jesus departing from Nazareth for the River Jordan and his baptism, and refer back to the earlier contemplations.

The sixth and following days

The unbeliever likes to think of the gospel as a myth, at best a useful morality tale. Well, if it pleases you start from that position. Read slowly through the Sermon on the Mount (Matthew chapters 5-7). Imagine that you are there. Read it again, don't immediately ask for faith and great things – or indeed anything. Let the message of the stories unfold slowly in your mind.

Again, the Rosary is a useful tool for quiet meditation. The five Sorrowful Mysteries of the Agony in the Garden, the Scourging at the Pillar, the Crowning with

Thorns, the Carrying of the Cross and the Crucifixion are marvellous paths in contemplation on how to cope with mental and physical pain, with derision and death in our own and others' lives.

Meditate on Jesus, his seclusion in the desert and his temptations. Ignatius follows on with various meditations. How St Andrew followed Christ; the Sermon on the Mount and the Beatitudes; how Christ appeared to his disciples; how he preached in the Temple and how he raised Lazarus. These can prolong the "week" into twelve days if you wish.

Ignatius then gives advice on how to make an *election*. He wants me to direct all my decisions in life to the service of God. He gives us this choice

> "To each and all he [Christ] issues his summons in these words: 'I am determined to bring under control the whole world and all my enemies, and so come to the glory of my Father. To anyone then who chooses to join me I offer nothing but a share in my hardships, but if he follows me in suffering he will assuredly follow me in glory'.'"

THE THIRD WEEK
OVERVIEW

In the third and fourth weeks the retreatant thinks through two opposites – The Passion of Jesus Christ and his Resurrection. Obviously, the theme in the third week must be sorrow for what we are witnessing, which will lead to a compassionate view of what is going on around us. The third week leads us quite actively for the personal sorrow we have felt in the first week. All this is helping us make the famous Ignatian Election between the different models of life which we can lead.

Again, as in the second week, we use Jesus' life as a guide for ourselves. For instance, as we prepare for the Last Supper, "The first prelude is to recall the *history*: how Christ our Lord sent two disciples from Bethany to Jerusalem to prepare the supper, and afterwards went there himself with the other disciples." But this again is not some distant historical event for us, it is in the here and now.

Then, in the third prelude, "To ask for what I want. Here it will be for grief, deep feeling and confusion because it is for my sins that the Lord is going to his Passion." So this story is personal for us. In a way, it is our fault it is happening at all.

Next, as we move forward in the story, we are there as an actual witness of the Last Supper. "The first point is to see the persons at the supper and by reflecting within myself to try and draw some profit from them."

The subjects to be contemplated throughout this week are divided into two parts. The first, as an exercise to be done at midnight, and the second in the morning.

> "At midnight, the subject of contemplation should be the events from the garden to the house of Annas, inclusive; in the morning from the house of Annas to the house of Caiaphas."

It is as if we are praying the Stations of the Cross. Here we witness the trial in front of Pilate through to the nailing on the cross. Then, at the end, we look at all the events.

The first day

Imagine a gospel theme, this time the road from Bethany to Jerusalem. Put your mind inside that of Christ, suffering with him as Judas prepares to betray him. Actually imagine the road – is it broad? Is it level? Sit yourself in the room of the Last Supper. Is it large or small, or arranged in one way or another?

At this point ask for regret, sorrow and confusion, "because the Lord is going to his Passion for your sins." Then look at and listen to the people present at the Last Supper.

Do a similar exercise as Jesus goes to the Garden of Gethsemane after the Supper, placing yourself there and describing it as you 'see' it. Ignatius asks us to pray "in sorrow, in company with Christ in his sorrow, being crushed with the pain that crushed Christ, tears, and a deep felt sense of suffering because Christ suffered so much for me."

The second day

Imagine the story of the Passion as it proceeds from the Garden to the House of Annas, and then on to the House of Caiaphas, the High Priest.

The third day

So onto the House of Pilate, again doing what you have done before, applying your senses and emotions to the scene. Perhaps imagining yourself on trial, being mocked and harassed.

The fourth day

Imagine the remaining scenes in front of Pilate.

The fifth day

Pass from Pilate to the Crucifixion and the death of Christ.

The sixth day

See Jesus taken down from the cross and laid in the tomb.

The seventh day

You can pass through all the events of the Passion, sharing Our Lady's grief with her, meditating upon the separation of Christ's body from His soul, and on to the place of His burial.

Throughout this week, Ignatius advises you to follow abstinence with regard to food.

THE FOURTH WEEK

We now, as in other weeks, meditate on all the mysteries of the Resurrection, up to and including the Ascension. Ignatius prescribes precise timings, near the noonday meal etc., and up to five meditations a day, but this can be varied as the retreatant wishes.

In the third week we have suffered with Christ. Now, in the fourth week, we join him in the joy, the very special type of joy which comes with an intense religious experience. This joy is no accident. We are, or perhaps should be, coming to believe that it is a form of grace given to us by Christ, because we are identifying with him and his life. The joy is the mood which we are to take with us out of the retreat.

Ignatius himself had a conversion experience, but he wants us to arise slowly from reasoned prayer and contemplation; not some sudden intense emotional experience that can fade away as quickly as it comes.

Again we follow the gospel stories. Thus in the "First Contemplation – How Christ our Lord appeared to our Lady", we are with Our Lady as she finds the tomb empty. Once again we are present at the scene. "The second prelude. Composition seeing the place. Here it will be to see the arrangement of the holy sepulchre, and the lodging or house of our Lady, looking in detail at all its parts, such as her room, oratory etc."

Towards the end of the fourth week, we arrive at St Ignatius' famous "Contemplation to Attain Love". This is the culmination of the Exercises. Here we are asked to find love in all things arising from our love for God and his love for us. Ignatius wants us in this exercise to look at our past, our world and our personal gifts, as we meet God bestowing his gifts upon us. Thus, in the "Second [Contemplation]: love consists in mutual communication. That is to say, the lover gives and communicates to the loved one what they have."

"The first prelude is the composition, which here is to see how I am before God our Lord, and the angels and the saints interceding for me."

"The second prelude. To ask for what I want. Here, it will be to ask for interior knowledge of all the good I have received, so that acknowledging this with gratitude, I may be able to love and serve his Divine Majesty in everything." We talk to God directly about what we want and about what he can give us, as a lover speaks to their loved one.

For Ignatius God is present in everything and is working at everything. "The third point. To consider, how God works and labours on my behalf in all created things on the face of the earth; that is, he acts in the manner of a person at work."

God is responsible for all the good in the world. "The fourth point. To see how all that is good and every gift descends from on high. Thus, my limited power descends from the supreme and infinite power above."

Ignatius now asks us to consider "Three ways of

praying". The first way would have been very traditional for this Renaissance man.

> "The first way of praying is concerned with the Ten Commandments and the Seven Deadly Sins, the Three Powers of the Soul and the Five Senses of the Body."

This we may find difficult, but it is at least intensely personal. It is about what we feel, what we have done or not done. The second way delves deeper into each prayer and the abundant wealth of prayer.

> "The second way of praying consists in contemplating the meaning of each word in a prayer."

Thus you could spend some time just on the first two words of the prayer "Our Father". The third way of praying is by rhythm and is influential in many types of meditation.

> "The third way of praying consists in praying mentally with each intake or expulsion of breath, by saying one word of the Our Father or of any prayer being said, so that only a single word is pronounced between one breath and the next. In the interval between each breath attention is especially paid to the meaning of that word."

Ignatius now lists scenes from the life of Christ upon which we can meditate on. Thus he refers to:

The Mysteries of the Life of Christ our Lord

The Annunciation

The Visitation

The Nativity

The Shepherds

The Circumcision

The Three Kings

The Purification of Our Lady and The Presentation

The Flight into Egypt

The Return of Our Lord from Egypt

The Life of Christ our Lord from the age
of twelve to the age of thirty

Christ's coming into the Temple
when he was aged twelve

The Baptism of Christ

The Temptations of Christ

The Call of the Apostles

The First Miracle performed
at the Marriage Feast of Cana

Christ our Lord drove the sellers out
of the Temple

The Sermon on the Mount

Christ our Lord Stilled the Tempest at Sea

Christ Our Lord Walking on the Sea

The Sending of the apostles to Preach

The Conversion of Magdalene

The Feeding by Christ of the Five Thousand

The Transfiguration of Christ

The Raising of Lazarus

The Supper at Bethany

Palm Sunday

The Preaching in the Temple

The Supper

The Mysteries Performed between
the Supper and the Garden

The Mysteries Performed between the Garden
and the House of Annas

The Mysteries Performed between the House
of Annas and the House of Caiaphas

The Mysteries Performed between the House
of Caiaphas and the House of Pilate

The Mysteries Performed between the House
of Pilate and the House of Herod

The Mysteries Performed between the House
of Herod and the House of Pilate

The Mysteries Performed between the House
of Pilate and the Cross

The Mysteries Performed on the Cross

The Mysteries Performed from the Cross
to the Tomb

The Resurrection of Christ our Lord
and the First Appearance

The Second to Thirteenth Appearance

The Ascension of Christ our Lord

As we ponder on all the things God has given us – our
very existence; our redemption and our own particular
gifts, realise that we should give up everything to him in
return, and say, "Take, Lord, and receive, all my liberty,
my memory, my understanding, and all my will – all that
I have and possess. You, Lord have given all that to me. I
now give it back to you. O Lord, all is Yours. Dispose of
it according to Your will. Give me love of Yourself along
with your grace, for that is enough for me."

Think of God dwelling in all the plants and creatures
of the earth, giving them their existence and conserving
them. Think also of goodness and justice descending
from God and thus your retreat draws to a close.

Meditation: The essence of this book

You will seek me and find me; when you seek me with all your heart. Jeremiah 29:13.

Part Two of this book has been about the Spiritual Exercises but, in this meditation, I want to show how the purpose of any spiritual exercise is to help us leave this life and confront God.

We will never proceed if we view prayer in purely personal terms. Prayer is putting oneself in the sight of God, approaching God not from the point of view of who we are, but something which is at once more interior, more hidden, more personal and also less constrained and tied to the individual.

For example, say we are called John Jones. Everything revolves around what people think of John Jones: how he is recognised, what work he does. Politicians, like myself, have this disease in an extreme measure. We get miffed if we have worked at something, led a crusade and the newspapers do not mention us by name. So, John Jones did not get any recognition today. So what?

This is not just the seething mind of John Jones, never at peace except in sleep and even then assailed by dreams, the mind jealous, resentful, plotting, relaxed for a moment because it has got what it wants but never happy until temporarily satiated. Who is John Jones? Although that is the name appended to a body his mind inhabits, is John Jones the only reality? We have to leap clear of the mind's John Jones.

A wonderful experience of the Ignatian route out of the usual mind of John Jones was granted me recently. I was walking in the Alps, a distant view of Mont Blanc behind me coming in and out of the clouds. The rain started to come down hard. I came to a small hamlet called Ormarets and took shelter in the tiny chapel. A mountain chapel capable of holding up to twenty or thirty people but empty now, of course. It housed a small wooden altar, ancient wooden statues of saints and old engravings of the Stations of the Cross on the walls. I sat there for a long time and then, very slowly, went round the stations, contemplating and praying each one. There was a commentary on the Mass readings for August at the back of the church. I read them. I suddenly realised that I had been alone in the chapel for nearly an hour. A profound joy and peace descended on my soul. Outside, the rain came and went, distant sounds of talking children came in the half-open door. I went on my way filled with happiness.

This was a spiritual exercise. They can come at anytime, anywhere. We just need to find a quiet place, to think, contemplate, and peace will come to us.

EPILOGUE

Politics is a rough trade, although perhaps not as rough as business. It is supposed to be about changing the world for the better. Too often it's about carving a position of power for oneself. It would be nice to say that my encounter with Ignatius transformed me from yet another career politician into a modern male version of Florence Nightingale. Sadly, that didn't happen. I haven't abandoned the world or its ambitions. The truth is more complex.

I said earlier that I was a religious person who found difficulty believing in God with no doubts whatever. I enjoy my religion; only I do not necessarily always believe in it as much as I would like to.

I take part in religious activities, not because I am a good person or a person who wants to do good, I am more selfish than most. I just *enjoy* it, and more than just in the sense in which one enjoys a good film or a bottle of wine. True, one can enjoy a beautiful church service on a purely aesthetic level, but the aesthetic appreciation is not an end in itself, it is a doorway to a pleasant spiritual plane, and a different world.

I engage in politics because I enjoy it, and because I am interested in it. An increasing interest in religion has not fundamentally changed my attitude to politics. I am no St Ignatius. I did not fall ill, read a religious book and decide to become a hermit in a cave or found a religious Order. However, for all that one's life goes on as before, something profound changes as a result of an Ignatian retreat.

It is not so much that one gets off the train and marches off in a different direction, but that the train journey is seen in proportion. It is no longer one's whole world. It may be uncomfortable or long, the train may not even be going precisely where one wants to go. One may have the dreary prospect of having to change and wait at a platform for a connection that doesn't come – or in the 'real world' of work or relationships, one may miss a connection in life, and the opportunity may never come back again. But, after making the Ignatian retreat, one can view these prospects with a certain equanimity.

I think of my career in politics as a middling failure rather than a half success. I have served twenty-nine years in parliament, sixteen years with my party in power, thirteen years in opposition, but I have spent twenty-six of those twenty-nine years on the back benches. If politics is power, then the power I have wielded has been brief and ephemeral. As a very junior minister at the Department of Trade and Industry, I achieved, I seem to remember, only two things. One was to ensure that when one buys an electrical appliance that it comes with a fitted plug. The other was to insist that when one bought a pint of beer, it really was a pint, with the froth on top of the beer and not below the top of the glass. The first 'achievement' has stood the test of time. The second was promptly overruled by a new Secretary of State, who had probably been got at by the brewers. In the end, none of this matters.

Very few politicians, even senior ministers who exercise real power, effect a great deal of change. Decisions on the issue of war and peace are probably the only occasions when individual politicians may change events in a decisive way. What was decided in August 1914 or September 1939 in Cabinet on the eve of war was vital, but who remembers what was in a budget ten or even five years ago?

I have failed, then, as a politician exercising power, but I believe ideas are more important. Out of the millions who lived in the nineteenth century, I remember very few – all those legions of generals and administrators of Empire, the proud recipients of honours and riches are all forgotten. I remember only a few men of ideas, a Darwin or a Marx, or people who gave their name to an era, like Queen Victoria.

So ideas are usually more important than actions. Mrs Thatcher will be remembered not so much for what she did, but because she represents the idea of privatisation of great state-owned interests. Gorbachev will be remembered not for what he did, but because he represents the idea of the collapse of Communist thought accompanying real power.

Of course, my career, along with that of most politicians, has been a failure in this respect too. Indeed, the Conservative MP Enoch Powell famously observed, "All political careers end in failure." Like any other politician, I have engaged in the current political debate, but anything I have said in Parliament will have been of little interest a few moments after I had said it.

In short, I have changed absolutely nothing. Equally, like most politicians, my life has not been a complete failure. I have played a role in scrutinising the executive. To use a cricketing metaphor, I have bowled a few overs and, if I haven't got anyone out, I have kept a few batsmen guessing. But I return to my central point. Has my religious experience changed anything?

I believe it has, in this sense: If what Christ told us is true, then Ignatius has to be right. It is of such importance that my only aim in life should be, can only be, to praise, reverence and serve God. Not just occasionally, in some formal setting in church on a Sunday, but every day – and several times a day at that.

The modern mind tends to view this as a rather sterile exercise, particularly if it is ritualised. It is as if to the modern person, God is just a sort of icon to worship, but if God really exists, He is in everything and is everywhere. As He said to Moses when He revealed Himself in the burning bush, "I AM WHO I AM." Therefore, I believe that we are part of this unity of being, although I understand it very imperfectly.

Thus, Ignatius' injunction has a profound effect on my day-to-day work. Like everyone else, I am normally full of angst about work. We all want to succeed or make a difference. We want to be respected and thought well of by others. But, although the world thinks this is natural and good, it is also (and I find it now) profoundly unsatisfactory. I am like a programmed robot which goes through these worldly motions, but my real self, my soul, views these actions as worthless.

The way of the world is in itself not necessarily wrong or selfish, but its pursuit makes one, and has made me, feel unhappy and ill at ease. We can achieve so much, but we are always a disappointment to ourselves, if not to others. We, or at least I, hit my own 'glass ceiling' in everything I do, and it is all too low. Thus, as I said earlier, I freely acknowledge that I have achieved little in the realm of ideas or of political action. But even those at the top of the political tree, the tiny minority who make it there, also feel frustrated. I believe most Prime Ministers, after seven years in office, or even Presidents of the United States after eight years, look into a mirror and say to themselves, "I've been given this tremendous unparalleled opportunity, and look what I've achieved: very little."

I think this feeling of underachievement arises in all professions. The artist is frustrated because he knows he is no Monet – or thinks he might have a chance of becoming one, if anyone would buy his paintings. Most actors are frustrated because they spend most of their time unemployed. They are bitter because they are not recognised, but even the famous actors we all hear about often lead very unhappy lives and remain dissatisfied with their work. Perhaps they feel they have wasted their talent on soaps and cop shows. Likewise, many novelists, successful men and women whose books sell in thousands, feel that too.

Forget about actors and artists and think of more humdrum professions. After a few years the same feelings of dissatisfaction arise in all of them. GPs are depressed after twenty years of listening to hypochondriacs in their surgeries; Civil servants are enmeshed in a web of stifling bureaucracy; businessmen are caught in a rat race and made redundant at the height of their powers; builders are under-employed; architects are not recognised, and so it goes on. I have not even mentioned yet the pressures of family life, or of millions of women forced to do unrewarding part-time work, with no prospects of promotion or recognition.

So, how on earth are all these people going to have more of a chance of leading fulfilled and happy lives? I believe they could do so – or at least make some progress towards this goal – by offering up their work to God every day. That they should think that everything they do is for God, not as a gift to a stranger, but to the created unity of which everyone is a part.

To put it in a homely English way, we are all part of a vast cricket team. Some people are more apparent at the moment, the batsmen and the bowlers, but around us are countless numbers of fielders, all concentrating on the same game. At any moment, they too will be asked to play their part.

Therefore, my belief in God does not make me lazy or laid-back (although one might be those things anyway). On the contrary, I am fully committed to a game in which, in reality, we are all on the same side, all on the same pitch and all under the same captain – God. That is why, to go back to the beginning of this story, Ignatius lying wounded in bed felt dissatisfied by reading tales of romance and chivalry, and why only religious reading of the lives of the saints left him feeling fulfilled. At that moment he encountered his destiny. In meditating on God, we too are encountering our destiny and will find true happiness – if we try.

AN ANSWER
TO THE GREATEST QUESTION

I said at the beginning of this book that I would try and answer the question I set myself – does God exist? This is my conclusion. We can never prove it and the attempt to do so is fundamentally a waste of time. The modern mind therefore revolts against the existence of God because it cannot accept anything that lacks obvious tangible existence or proof. However, this leaves a residue of terrible, if unconscious, angst in us. We know we are going to die and we can take nothing with us. What is it all for?

My conclusion is this: we should assume God exists, not try and determine whether he does or not. We should throw ourselves off the precipice of faith without any means of knowing if there is a safety net of truth to break the fall. If we assume that God exists, and then assume that the gospels are the literal truth, a wonderful thing will happen – our lives will be transformed. But, we really have to make that assumption and live our lives accordingly. So many questions will be answered. How glorious that every motion we make, and that is made around us, is held in loving embrace by an eternal God. We need never fear again.

Therefore, my first resolution of this problem is not to waste one's life trying to prove an unprovable point, but to assume it. My second conclusion is that having made the assumption, it will become impossible to sustain if we just become – or remain – Sunday Christians, going to church once a week, muttering maybe a hasty prayer in trouble. We should become monks in the wider world. This is my concept of the 'Open Monastery'. We have to have a routine of prayer on rising, perhaps saying the Divine Office through the month, working our way through all the psalms; of attending, if possible, a daily communal act of worship and saying our evening prayer, as well as daily spiritual reading. We should also offer up our work to God. This is a Benedictine way of balance between work, study and prayer all through the day, interweaving prayer into our daily work. We should become monks, not of the cloister, but monks of the wider world with a family.

Often we will fail in our resolution, but if we persist, marvellous gifts will be vouchsafed to us. Our life will be transformed.

2·50